"This may be the best and r
the subject of Satan. Only J
the devil and make it fun and incredibly informative."

—Steve Brown, founder of Key Life and author
of *Laughter and Lament*

"A wild ride! This book had me laughing, gawking, and crying on the same page. Timely, witty, essential truth for what ails us. If you shake your head in disbelief at a world gone mad, this book will make a whole lot of sense and equip you to do something about it."

—Danielle Strickland, author of *The Other Side of Hope* and
host of the *Right Side Up* podcast

"Jared Brock has no sympathy for the devil, but my goodness—he's written both a riveting biography and a sweeping exposé of Old Scratch, and on top of that compiled a comprehensive manual of defense tactics to withstand Satan's wiles. It's a daunting task to tackle such a grim subject, but Jared does it with characteristic wit, wisdom, flair, and—above all—love for the church. This is, in fact, mostly that: an extended epistle to the people of God on how not to be unaware of the devil's schemes. In *A Devil Named Lucifer*, Jared Brock gives us the evil one's entire playbook. We're well armed."

—Mark Buchanan, author of THE DAVID TRILOGY

"Sometimes controversial, always thought-provoking, and full of carefully researched insight."

—Christopher Frost, Christian YouTuber

"With passion, conviction, wit, and creativity, Jared unpacks a widely familiar but misunderstood adversary. I was wide-eyed from the start as the identification of his tactics in daily life was applied time and time again. This book will serve you and the church well, now and in years to come."

—Matthew Naismith, national director of C3 Canadian Campus Collective, host of *The Sowers* podcast, and church-planting catalyst with Send Network Canada

"Jared Brock has done it again. A robust yet approachable book on the devil. This is no easy feat. Jared gives lyrical light to a topic entirely bent on deceptive darkness. We must know the enemy we are at war with. Equip yourself by reading this application-rich book."

—James Kelly, founder and CEO of FaithTech

A DEVIL NAMED LUCIFER

BOOKS BY JARED BROCK

A Devil Named Lucifer
A God Named Josh
The Road to Dawn
Bearded Gospel Men
A Year of Living Prayerfully

A DEVIL NAMED LUCIFER

Uncovering the
Diabolical Life of Satan and
How to Resist Him

JARED BROCK

BETHANYHOUSE
a division of Baker Publishing Group
Minneapolis, Minnesota

© 2025 by Jared Brock

Published by Bethany House Publishers
Minneapolis, Minnesota
BethanyHouse.com

Bethany House Publishers is a division of
Baker Publishing Group, Grand Rapids, Michigan

Printed in the United States of America

Library of Congress Cataloging-in-Publication Data
Names: Brock, Jared, author.
Title: A devil named Lucifer : uncovering the diabolical life of satan and how to
    resist him / Jared Brock.
Description: Minneapolis, Minnesota : Bethany House, a division of Baker
    Publishing Group, 2025. | Includes bibliographical references.
Identifiers: LCCN 2024041231 | ISBN 9780764240485 (paper) | ISBN 9780764242724
    (casebound) | ISBN 9781493445127 (ebook)
Subjects: LCSH: Devil—History of doctrines. | Devil—History. | Christian life.
Classification: LCC BT982 .B734 2025 | DDC 235/.47—dc23/eng/20241028
LC record available at https://lccn.loc.gov/2024041231

Unless otherwise indicated, Scripture quotations are from The Holy Bible, English Standard Version® (ESV®), copyright © 2001 by Crossway, a publishing ministry of Good News Publishers. Used by permission. All rights reserved. ESV Text Edition: 2016

Scripture quotations labeled KJV are from the King James Version of the Bible.

Scripture quotations labeled NIV are from THE HOLY BIBLE, NEW INTERNATIONAL VERSION®, NIV® Copyright © 1973, 1978, 1984, 2011 by Biblica, Inc.® Used by permission. All rights reserved worldwide.

The image of the devil in chapter 4 was generated by DALL·E 3, OpenAI, at https://www.bing.com/images/create/.

Emojis are from the open-source library OpenMoji (https://openmoji.org/) under the Creative Commons license CC BY-SA 4.0 (https://creativecommons.org/licenses/by-sa/4.0/legalcode).

Cover design by Micah Kandros Design

Baker Publishing Group publications use paper produced from sustainable forestry practices and postconsumer waste whenever possible.

25 26 27 28 29 30 31   7 6 5 4 3 2 1

This book is dedicated to Chris and Kate Frost
for their angelic hospitality that made this book possible.

CONTENTS

PREFACE

My mother and siblings left early for Guelph Bible Chapel because Mom was on coffee duty. I was supposed to ride with my father, who was the church's youth pastor and due to teach Sunday school in fifteen minutes. "I'm just on a quick phone call," he whispered. "We'll leave in five minutes."

Ten minutes later, I ran into Dad's office. "You're going to be late for class!" I said. My father, wide-eyed, covered the receiver. "Go downstairs and pray—I'm on the phone with a demon."

My twelve-year-old self rushed downstairs to my bedroom, where I dropped on my knees and clasped my hands in prayer. *Dear God . . . please . . . umm . . . slay the demon?* I stumbled through a perfectly incoherent prayer, unsure what to say or think. My mind was reeling. Dad's on the phone with a demon? What are they talking about? Since when do demons own phones?

I doubt I said twenty words of prayer before sneaking back upstairs to listen at Dad's office door. It was mostly silent—clearly the thing on the other end of the phone was doing most of the chin-wagging. I paced back and forth for a small eternity, alternating between prayer-mutters and eavesdropping. I wondered who would police the several dozen rowdy teenage boys whose Sunday school teacher had canceled class without notice.

An hour later, it was over. We had properly missed church for the first time in living memory. "You can come in," Dad said. I burst into the room, flopped down on his black leather recliner, and started my inquisition.

"Tell me everything."

INTRODUCTION:
SPEAK OF THE DEVIL

We have never heard the devil's side of the story—
God wrote all the books.

—Attributed to Anatole France

In my previous book, *A God Named Josh*, I set out to myth-bust the life of Jesus Christ by showing scripturally how Jesus was actually named Yehoshua ben Yehoseph, how He likely wasn't born at Christmas, likely worked with stone instead of wood, had far more than twelve disciples (many of whom were women), and wasn't killed by "the Jews," but was actually assassinated due to the machinations of a money-hungry crime family. The goal was to help readers envision a more accurate image of Jesus so we could walk in His footsteps a little less waveringly.

I hope to do something similar regarding Satan in *A Devil Named Lucifer*. When you understand how he works, why he does what he does, and who he does it for, it makes life's challenges easier to bear.

But let me tell you, writing a book about the devil is significantly harder than writing a book about Jesus. For one thing, the Bible barely mentions the brute, whereas every page of Scripture is about Jesus. Books, articles, films, and other research on the devil only provide so much help, usually with a heaping helping of added confusion and unclarity. If anything, there are more volumes of misinformation and disinformation on the devil than hard facts. So most Christians are left confused, and pastors typically just avoid preaching on the devil altogether. That is, unless the pastor or televangelist is downright obsessed with the devil, in which case they inflate the devil far more than he deserves or warrants.

Indeed, the devil is an extremely popular fellow.

Just think of how many idioms there are about him: The devil is in the details. The devil makes work for idle hands. Better the devil you know. When someone we like (or dislike) walks into the room we say, "Speak of the devil." We describe a blue or red politician as "The devil incarnate." When it's time to pay up, we "give the devil his due." When we want to present the opposing side of an argument, we "play devil's advocate."

We humans love to name objects in his honor, too. Case in point: I live near a Devil's Bridge, and I used to live near a Devil's Punchbowl. All over the world, there are big, scary Devil's Dykes, Devil's Slides, Devil's Gorges, Devil's Dens, Devil's Hills, Devil's Valleys, Devil's Canyons, Devil's Towers, and even a Devil's Throat and Devil's Nostrils.

What the devil is going on? How can a being who gets roughly three mentions in the Old Testament, is flicked away like a fly by Jesus in the New Testament, and utterly trounced by God in Revelation get so much airtime and headspace in the life of Christians and the wider culture?

What's most intriguing about the devil is how remarkably steady Christian belief in him has remained over the millennia. Christendom has shifted its stance on so many issues—salvation, church structure, head coverings, you name it—but for all the changes, corrections, innovations, and heresies that have swirled around the Christian church for the past 2,000 years, the Christian doctrine of the devil has remained remarkably unchanged. The Council of Braga in 563 laid out what is essentially the popular belief held today. The Fourth Lateran Council in 1215 and the Council of Trent in 1546 fine-tuned a few bits and bobs, as did the Catholic Catechism in 1992, but on the whole, our Satanology has barely wavered from beliefs set down a millennia and a half ago.

We live in polarized times, don't we? One is either a vegan or a carnivore, on the side of Israel or Palestine, a corporatist Democrat or a corporatist Republican. So, too, are we made to choose sides as to the existence of the devil and his nature. Is he the physical embodiment of evil or simply a symbol of it? Does he live in heaven or hell?

The questions surrounding the devil are virtually endless. In this book, we'll try to tackle some of them, including:

What's the difference between hell, Hades, Sheol, and the lake of fire, and where exactly are they?

Why is the devil considered the embodiment of evil when the Bible never describes him that way?

Are angels and demons real? How many are there? Can angels become demons and vice versa?

What is Lucifer's real name? Is it first name Satan, last name Devil—or the other way around?

Why is the devil called Lucifer even though that word never appears in the original language of the Bible?

What happens if I've made a Faustian bargain or deal with the devil?

Why does the angel of God appear as a satan in Numbers 22:22?

Can Christians be demon possessed, oppressed, or repressed?

Why is Jesus basically called a "lucifer" in 2 Peter 1:19?

Who is the antichrist? How many antichrists are there?

Are Satan and the Eden serpent the same being?

What is the unpardonable sin?

What's the deal with 666?

We've got lots to cover, so here's where we're headed:

In chapter 1, we'll discover the devil's name isn't actually Lucifer.

In chapter 2, we'll discover the devil's name isn't actually Satan.

In chapter 3, we'll discover the devil's name isn't actually even Devil, and we'll give him a new and hopefully more helpful English name.

In chapter 4, we'll tear up the trope-packed picture we have of the devil—really rip the silly snapshot to shreds—and then try to re-paint his original portrait with a far finer brush.

In chapter 5, we'll dive deeply into the demonic and see who we're up against.

In chapter 6, we'll create a spiritual org chart to help us visualize heaven's hierarchy and the devil's place in it.

In chapter 7, we'll walk through the devil's powers and lack of power.

In chapter 8, we'll discuss how to spot, avoid, and overcome the devil's tests, tricks, and tactics.

In chapter 9, our longest, we'll unpack the problem of evil and try to reconcile the idea of a loving God allowing a world of hate.

In chapter 10, we'll learn how we can use the devil to serve God. This is a big one. Christians can actually profitably use the devil to their personal spiritual benefit and the advancement of God's kingdom. (As we'll see in one case in the Bible, God even uses the devil to lead someone to salvation.)

In chapter 11, we'll dive into the apocalyptic Revelation and the end of days.

In chapter 12, we'll discover the devil's future, and more important, our post-devil eternity.

Along the way, we'll try to dispel some major myths, such as the idea that the devil lives in hell. We'll erase the image we have of him—red face, sharp horns, pointy goatee, etc.—and craft a more biblical portrait. We'll also discuss the erroneous notion that the devil is Christ's opposite but equal. Last but certainly not least, we'll consider the major question that forms part of any discussion regarding the devil: How could a truly loving and all-powerful God allow evil, sin, death, and the devil to inflict suffering on innocent men, women, and children? All that and much more in the pages ahead.

Getting eyeglasses as a boy provided a before-and-after moment for my vision and my outlook on the world. My aim with this book is similar—not to deconstruct the devil but to clarify him. The Bible itself doesn't change, but our fuzzy reading of it needs a sharper prescription. You might be wondering if and why any of this matters. It does, and here's why: A truly biblical under-standing of the devil is vital for many reasons, the most important of which is that it helps clarify our understanding of God. Could the stakes be any higher?

Here's an example: If a Christian believes the devil is the source of all evil, then humans are not actually to be blamed for their sins. And if God then punishes these technically innocent people for sinning, then He is not just, holy, and perfect, and is therefore not God.

Here's another: If a Christian believes the devil is God's op-posite but equal and the universe is just an evenly matched battle between good and evil, then Christianity is nothing more than a

Neo-Zoroastrian dualist cult. Is the fate of humanity really up for grabs? Can God really protect us? Can we trust He is working all things together for our good?

And another: If a Christian believes God created the devil as the personification of evil, then God created evil. This is a straight-up heresy.

One more: If a Christian believes the devil's real name is Lucifer, then they've accidentally given him a name that *rightfully belongs to Jesus.*

As you can see, a proper Satanology is extremely important if we want to live as biblically faithful followers of Jesus. That's why this book is grounded in biblical truth—and designed to drive you to Scripture. Please don't take my word on anything written in the pages that follow. Have a Bible ready at all times, as this book contains nearly 2,000 Scripture references so you can see for yourself that I'm not just making this stuff up as I go along. I'm merely a messenger, a fellow pilgrim on the Way. What's truly wild about the devil is that the Bible contains his entire biography—his past, present, *and* future. His story and demise are already written in the heavens. My job is simply to help you better understand it.

My highest goal for this book is to help you see the massive brilliance of Jesus and joyfully accept the absolute sovereignty of God's kingship over all things. The hope is to reveal His ultimate plan for the universe and our role in that epic story. These insights will radically reshape how we view the devil and his work in our lives, as well as elevate our sense of meaning, purpose, and mission in the face of seemingly ever-growing evil. I hope you walk away from this book feeling new hope and anticipation for the future.

Oh, and one more thing: The devil is furious that you're reading this. Expect obstacles, challenges, setbacks, struggles, and strife to keep you from finishing. The last thing the devil needs is another person who sees who and what he really is, who understands how small and weak he is compared with God, who is keenly aware of his devices (2 Corinthians 2:11), and who knows how to use him to fulfill God's purposes. **Expect resistance.** This book is an unauthorized biography. To my knowledge, the subject has refused to cooperate and, as you will see in the postscript, he seems to have put up quite the fight against exposure. He will likely do the same with you.

My suggestion? Don't fight alone. Read this book with a friend, a family member, or a small group. Make notes along the way on the lined pages at the back of this book. Pray before and after you read and discuss each chapter. The enemy is real, and a fellow warrior in Christ's heavenly army can be a major help in your defense.

Jared Brock
Ceredigion, Wales
January 2024

PART I

WHAT'S HIS NAME?

1

LUCIFER

"Lucifer, oh, Lucifer
The darkness is where you find your light."

—Kenneth Gamble, Alexander Chiger, Andre Harris,
Chris Bridges, Harry Zelnick, Leon Huff, Vidal Davis,
"War with God"

IN 1828, AN ENGLISH CHEMIST named Samuel Jones patented a small sulfur-coated splinter of wood dipped in gum, potassium chlorate, and antimony sulfide. When struck against any rough surface such as a rock, sandpaper, or metal, the tiny bulbous friction stick would instantly burst into flame. The fire it produced was smelly, smoky, and toxic, but the masses loved it, and Jones made a fortune. Jones patented his strike-anywheres, now known in English as *matches*, using a Latin word: *lucifer*.

The French, German, and Swedish words for match—*allumette*, *streichholz*, and *tändsticka*—all derive from lucifer. The Dutch didn't even bother to create a Dutch word—in the Netherlands, a lucifer is just a lucifer.

The word *lucifer* comes from the Latin *lux* (light) and *fer* (bearing), and it wasn't only used as the name for Samuel Jones's friction match. Take, for instance, the planet Venus. It's the third-brightest object in our sky after the sun and the moon. When Venus appeared as the evening star after sunset, the ancient Romans called it *vesper*. (If you've ever attended a candlelit evening prayer service at a monastery—highly recommended—you've taken part in vespers.) When Venus appeared before sunrise as the morning star, however, the Romans gave Venus a different name: *lucifer*. Venus brought the sun to the sunrise, ergo, Venus was the light-bringing lucifer.

Our original Old Testament, written in Hebrew, and the New Testament written in Greek, never use the Latin word *lucifer*, of course. But in an early Latin translation of the Bible called the Vulgate, the Greek word *phósphoros* is translated as the Latin *lucifer*.

Getting back to matches, early twentieth-century matches were made using highly toxic white phosphorus, causing thousands of workers—mostly teenage girls and destitute young women—to contract phossy jaw, an excruciating and disfiguring disease that caused fistulas, abscesses, and a putrid rotting of the jaw that made people's bones glow greenish-white. Today's matches are made with red phosphorus, a more expensive but much safer variety popularized by the Salvation Army's 1891 match-making factory. Finland was the first country to ban white phosphorus in 1872, but Britons didn't bother to start protecting their people until 1910—and the last British factory that produced white phosphorus matches didn't close until 1970.

Match history aside, being a lucifer is a wonderful thing. Who wouldn't want to share Christ and reflect His glory to the world? Who wouldn't want to be a light-bringer to the darkness of Kolkata's brothels or a light-bearer to the nation-devouring banks of Wall Street and the City of London?

The apostle Peter (Jesus's lead disciple, Cephas) more or less calls Jesus a lucifer in 2 Peter 1:19—"We have the prophetic word more fully confirmed, to which you will do well to pay attention

24

as to a lamp shining in a dark place, until the day dawns and the morning star [Greek *phósphoros*/Latin *lucifer*] rises in your hearts."

This English term *morning star* appears a few other times in the ESV Bible.

In Job 38:7, God asks Job about the establishment of the foundations of the earth "when the morning stars sang together and all the sons of God shouted for joy." Commentators mostly agree YHWH is talking about physical stars and heavenly angels here. The Hebrew phrase used is *boqer kowkbe*.

In Revelation 2:28, Jesus promises to give the "morning star" (Greek *astera ton prōinon*) to those who hold fast until the end.

Who is this morning star? In Revelation 22:16, Jesus makes the big reveal: Jesus says that *He* is the "bright morning star" (Greek *aster ho lampros ho prōinos*). If anyone in the Bible has the right to be called a light-bearing Latin lucifer, it's Jesus.

Isaiah 14:12 contains a similar term: "How you are fallen from heaven, O Day Star [Hebrew *helel*], son of Dawn! How you are cut down to the ground, you who laid the nations low!" In case there's any confusion about who's being talked about here, YHWH makes it clear in Isaiah 14:4. "You will take up this taunt against the king of Babylon." What follows is a verbal victory dance, a satire by the house of Israel against their former captor. That is, until things get weird in the verses after Isaiah 14:12. "You said in your heart, 'I will ascend to heaven; above the stars of God I will set my throne on high; I will sit on the mount of assembly in the far reaches of the north; I will ascend above the heights of the clouds; I will make myself like the Most High.'"

It leaves the Israelite taunter wondering, "Are we still laying a dope smackdown on the king of Babylon or is this razz actually about the spiritual force *behind* either Sargon II, Nabonidus, or Belshazzar?" The latter is the conclusion reached by early Christian writers such as Origen and Jerome, that this taunt is actually against the devil and not just a despotic warlord.

Isaiah 14:12 might be drawing on a Canaanite myth about a god named Helel. His name means morning star, and he's the son of El, the father of all gods. In the Canaanite story, Helel is hurled into Sheol, thanks to his attempt to enthrone himself above his father. Sound familiar? Isaiah may be using a local myth to mock the soon-to-fall king of Babylon, but that doesn't necessarily mean this is the devil's own origin story. Either way, Lucifer is absolutely and equivocally *not* the proper name of the devil. To Christianity's credit, eminent folks like Augustine and Gregory the Great strongly disagreed with Origen and Jerome's interpretation and said so, but much later writers like Dante and Milton doubled down on Lucifer and made the name permanently stick in the popular imagination.

How did this happen? How did a name reserved for Jesus and His holy angels get applied to the devil himself? As pointed out previously, the original Hebrew word for Day Star, or Morning Star, in Isaiah 14:12 is *helel*. It just means "a shining one." A luminary, a leading light. We still call actors "movie stars" and elite athletes "superstars." But the Latin Vulgate translated Isaiah 14:12 as "Quomodo cecidisti de caelo, lucifer, fili aurorae?" "How have you fallen from heaven, O Lucifer, son of the dawn?" And there it is. Despite the fact that the devil is absolutely not a lucifer, and is never called a lucifer even once in the original Bible, he is now officially a devil named Lucifer. (At the risk of furthering the confusion, I've entitled this book *A Devil Named Lucifer* not because that's his actual name, but because that's what people have named him.) Aren't humans strange? Through translation and transliteration we turned Yehoshua ben Yehoseph into "Jesus," and we turned a description of Jesus into the name of the devil.

Notice what a lucifer is not. A lucifer is not a light itself. A lucifer is not a light-generator. It's just a carrier, a transmitter, a steward. A lucifer simply reflects the light of Christ the way the moon reflects the light of the sun. The Latin Vulgate translation has three other mentions of a lucifer (all lowercase) in addition to the light-bringers of Isaiah 14:12 and 2 Peter 1:19. In Job 11:17, the lucifer is the brightness that will shine on Job once he gets through his dark night of the soul. In Job 38:32, the lucifer is God's glorious constellations in the night sky. In Psalm 109:3, in the Latin Vulgate (Psalm 110:3 in English Bibles), the lucifer is the radiant brightness of God's glory reflecting off the saints of His army.

In other words, even in the Latin Vulgate, all five mentions of a lucifer have nothing to do with the devil.

Christ? Lucifer.
Creation? Lucifer.
Christians? Lucifers.
The devil? *Not Lucifer.*

Friends, the word *lucifer* **doesn't appear even once in the majority of modern Bibles** and for good reason: It causes major confusion among Christians and non-Christians alike. In reality, Jesus is the true lucifer who lights the path to God. Jesus is the source of light who brings hope to the world. Christ's angels, too, are the lucifers who bear His light, as is the luminosity of nature itself, a notion stunningly captured in Psalm 19:1; Isaiah 40:26; and Romans 1:20. Christians, last but not least, are the light-bearing lucifers tasked with radiating the inner light of Christ, illuminating the path to Jesus, and bringing evermore glory to our radiant King. In case you have any doubt whether God wants you to be a light-radiating superstar Christian, check out Daniel 12:3. "Those who are wise shall shine like the brightness of the sky above; and those who turn many to righteousness, like the stars forever and ever." If a minister really wanted to wake up their congregation, they could do no better than to end next Sunday's service with a benediction based on 2 Peter 1:19. *May you stand faithful until day dawns and the true "Lucifer" rises in your hearts.*

Still, there's some truth to the feeling that the Isaiah 14 passage is about more than a mere Mesopotamian monarch, isn't there? Like much of the Bible, the possibility of a double meaning seems to reveal itself in the text. Isaiah 14:13–14 brilliantly encapsulates the twisted luciferian aspiration that all kings and other tyrannical despots hope to achieve. Rather than basking in the light of God's glory and bearing it to others, they (we?) want to become the source itself.

It's never a great idea to boast about our plans for the future (Proverbs 27:1; James 4:13–16; Luke 12:16–21) but in just two verses, the king of Babylon (and perhaps the devil, and you and I) makes five "I will" declarations that he cannot possibly keep.

1. "I will ascend to heaven; above the stars of God."

   In other words, the king/devil firstly wants to be ranked above all the angels. The author of Hebrews 2:9 notes how Jesus does the *opposite* of the devil in fulfilling the Psalm 8:5 prophecy: "But we see him who for a little while was made lower than the angels, namely Jesus, crowned with glory and honor because of the suffering of death, so that by the grace of God he might taste death for everyone." We want to ascend, but Christ condescends.

2. "I will set my throne on high."

   The king/devil wants supreme power. A global empire from whence to reign as king of kings and lord of lords. Jesus in John 18:36 tells Pilate that He desires no earthly throne: "My kingdom is not of this world. If my kingdom were of this world, my servants would have been fighting, that I might not be delivered over to the Jews. But my kingdom is not from the world."

3. "I will sit on the mount of assembly in the far reaches of the north."

   Kings and devils require prestigious palaces, elevated pedestals, penthouse suites, and corner offices. Jesus, on the other hand, doesn't require a stage or platform. "Foxes have holes, and birds of the air have nests, but the Son of Man has nowhere to lay his head" (Matthew 8:20).

4. "I will ascend above the heights of the clouds."

Kings and devils aren't satisfied with mere earthly rule. Their domain must extend over time and space, achieving "immortality" through godlike acts of war, writing, and construction. Jesus never bothered to conquer new lands, write a boastful biography of His triumphs, or build a single pillar or colosseum in His own memory. Jesus didn't ascend. He came down to us. And He may have descended even further—some theologians believe that 1 Peter 4:6; Romans 10:6–7; and Ephesians 4:9–10 suggest Jesus went so low as to visit Hades, but it's far from absolute.*

5. "I will make myself like the Most High."

Please note that even the devil wants to be like God. Isn't that strange? He doesn't want to be *un*-Godlike. He wants to be Godlike. Of course he knows he can never be God, but he thinks he can negotiate for the next best things—autonomy, independence, self-sufficiency—all things we humans can never achieve. Kings and devils want God's three omnis: omnipotence (all the power), omniscience (all the knowledge), and omnipresence (to experience everything everywhere all at once). We and the devil can have exactly none of them. So what does the devil do? He dupes the world into thinking he's equal in power to God. This belief, this myth of God

---

* Here's another really fun one from 1 Peter 3:18–20 in the NIV. "For Christ also suffered once for sins, the righteous for the unrighteous, to bring you to God. He was put to death in the body but made alive in the Spirit. After being made alive, he went and made proclamation to the imprisoned spirits—to those who were disobedient long ago when God waited patiently in the days of Noah while the ark was being built." Is this text suggesting Jesus went to Hades or Sheol or hell? Perhaps. Did he time-travel back to Noah's day? Intriguing but unlikely. Was the Holy Spirit already working through Noah to draw people to God? This seems to me to be the most likely of all scenarios.

versus Satan, good-versus-evil cosmic dualism, is not a biblical Christian belief at all, but bad theology that seeped into Christendom via Persian Zoroastrianism.

And what does Jesus want during His time on earth? Surprise, surprise. The opposite of what kings and devils crave. Christ Jesus, "who, though he was in the form of God, did not count equality with God a thing to be grasped, but emptied himself, by taking the form of a servant, being born in the likeness of men. And being found in human form, he humbled himself by becoming obedient to the point of death, even death on a cross" (Philippians 2:6–8). While on earth, Jesus is happy to play the role of the light-bearing lucifer and humbly take His instructions from God. "I can do nothing on my own. As I hear, I judge, and my judgment is just, because I seek not my own will but the will of him who sent me" (John 5:30).

Isn't Jesus positively gorgeous? John uses the word *light* seven times in John 1:4–9, and is clear that the light is Jesus, yet even Jesus doesn't try to distract from God the Father. Like the earthly Jesus, we should all endeavor to become lucifers—light-bearers who carry and reflect the one Source of all light. But like the devil and despots throughout history, we must never make the fatal error of trying to make ourselves the Light itself.

For those who might be starting to get worried, it is in no way my intention to deconstruct the devil or Christianity. Quite the opposite. We should demolish the nonbiblical devil of popular culture and return to the devil who actually appears in the Bible, so Christians can be strengthened to advance the kingdom of our Lord. We must know the *real* enemy. Now that we've made our valiant attempt to put to bed the millennia-old myth that the devil's name is Lucifer, let's set our sights and do the same to his next most culturally popular name: Satan.

2

SATAN

"The devil's agents may be of flesh and blood, may they not?"
—Arthur Conan Doyle, *The Hound of the Baskervilles*

IF YOU THOUGHT THE NAME LUCIFER was tricky, wait until you see what's up with Satan.

The Hebrew word *satan* first appears in written history around the seventh century BC. The text is 1 Samuel 29:4, and it is decidedly *not* about the devil. It is in reference to David: "But the commanders of the Philistines were angry with him. And the commanders of the Philistines said to him, 'Send the man [David] back, that he may return to the place to which you have assigned him. He shall not go down with us to battle, lest in the battle he become an adversary [*satan*] to us.'"

So the first chronological use of *satan* in the Bible refers to David, who is described in 1 Samuel 13:14 and Acts 13:22 as a man after God's own heart.

That said, while 1 Samuel 29:4 might be the first *satan* written down, the first mention of *satan* in the current order of our Bibles occurs in Numbers 22:22. In this case as well, the *satan* in question is not the devil; it is the angel of God: "But God's anger was kindled because he went, and the angel of the LORD took his stand in the way as his adversary [*satan*]."

Okay, so the first two satans in Scripture refer to a godly dude and God's personal dude. *Satan* doesn't mean wicked or evil or violent or sinful. A satan is an adversary. But, as we shall see, there's also *the* Adversary, a being with particularly adversarial tendencies. The word can be used with the definite article (the satan), indefinite article (a satan), and as a proper name (Satan). Here's a strange but true sentence: Satan was a satan and he sataned. Adversary was an adversary and he acted adversarially.

The first undeniable Satan with a capital S isn't seen until Job 1:6, a full 417 pages into my Bible.* However, even in this passage, the word *Satan* is preceded by the definite article. It's "the Satan," not "Satan." The first capital-S Satan is an appellative, a description. The Satan. That's not to say Job 1:6 isn't talking about Satan. Many scholars are convinced it is. When one mentions the Rock today, they are surely talking about the movie star Dwayne Johnson. When someone mentions the Donald, who else but President Trump comes to mind? The King . . . Elvis Presley. The Edge . . . U2's guitarist. You get the idea. The Satan of Job 1:6 might very well refer to the devil himself. Let's see this devil in action:

The book of Job starts by introducing us to a godly man from Uz (likely somewhere in the Levant). He has ten adult children,

---

* Fellow Bible nerds will note that 1 Chronicles 21:1 also mentions "the Satan," but it's a variated parallel of 2 Samuel 24:1 that leaves some scholars wondering if the chronicler perhaps edited the verse for clarity. Thus, my assertion that Job 1:6 is the first clear and explicit mention of the Satan with a capital S. The verse in 2 Samuel 24:1 reads, "Again the anger of the LORD was kindled against Israel, and he incited David against them, saying, 'Go, number Israel and Judah.'" Clearly, Israel had disobeyed and was in need of discipline and correction. But God, being merciful, offers David a trust test. David fails miserably. He even ignores a warning from Joab to trust Yahweh. The military census allowed David to put his trust in his 1.3 million troops instead of his infinitely more powerful God. It was yet another act of human self-reliance instead of God-reliance, and it led to the death of 70,000 people.

11,000 animals, and tons of employees. Nice to meet you, Job from Uz. In verse 6, the scene switches to heaven:

> Now there was a day when the sons of God came to present themselves before the LORD, and [the Adversary] also came among them. The LORD said to [the Adversary], "From where have you come?" [The Adversary] answered the LORD and said, "From going to and fro on the earth, and from walking up and down on it." And the LORD said to [the Adversary], "Have you considered my servant Job, that there is none like him on the earth, a blameless and upright man, who fears God and turns away from evil?" Then [the Adversary] answered the LORD and said, "Does Job fear God for no reason? Have you not put a hedge around him and his house and all that he has, on every side? You have blessed the work of his hands, and his possessions have increased in the land. But stretch out your hand and touch all that he has, and he will curse you to your face." And the LORD said to [the Adversary], "Behold, all that he has is in your hand. Only against him do not stretch out your hand." So [the Adversary] went out from the presence of the LORD.

> Job 1:6–12

So, the Adversary obediently heads to earth to test Job's faithfulness to God. In verse 15, he convinces the Sabeans to murder a bunch of Job's employees. In verse 16, the fire of God falls from heaven and burns up the sheep and more employees. In verse 17, the Chaldeans murder and steal whatever's left of Job's holdings. In verse 19, a heavy wind flattens the house in which all ten of Job's kids are feasting. Job's response to these four horrific reports is the stuff of legends: He stands up, tears his robe, shaves his head, and falls on the ground in worship. "Naked I came from my mother's womb, and naked shall I return. The Lord gave, and the Lord has taken away; blessed be the name of the Lord" (Job 1:21).

Picking up in Job 2,

Again there was a day when the sons of God came to present themselves before the LORD, and [the Adversary] also came among them to present himself before the LORD. And the LORD said to [the Adversary], "From where have you come?" [The Adversary] answered the LORD and said, "From going to and fro on the earth, and from walking up and down on it." And the LORD said to [the Adversary], "Have you considered my servant Job, that there is none like him on the earth, a blameless and upright man, who fears God and turns away from evil? He still holds fast his integrity, although you incited me against him to destroy him without reason." Then [the Adversary] answered the LORD and said, "Skin for skin! All that a man has he will give for his life. But stretch out your hand and touch his bone and his flesh, and he will curse you to your face." And the LORD said to [the Adversary], "Behold, he is in your hand; only spare his life."

So [the Adversary] went out from the presence of the LORD.

Job 2:1–7

The Adversary strikes Job with sores from head to toe. Job takes to scraping his sores with a piece of broken pottery while sitting in an ash heap. His wife suggests he should curse God and die. Three very good friends join him in a week of silent mourning. Chapters 3 through 27 contain an emotional rollercoaster of dialogue between Job and his friends and Job and God about the nature of evil and suffering. Job works his way through the five stages of grief, but there is no satisfying conclusion or definitive answer as to why bad things happen to seemingly good people. Job learns that not all suffering is punishment but is sometimes just a test of faithfulness in God and trust in His sovereignty. The story has a happy earthly ending for Job, at least—not only does he remain faithful, but God blesses him with 22,000 animals and ten new kids, and he even lived long enough to know his great-grandkids.

But where did Satan go? After initiating Job's test, the Adversary simply disappears from the story. Who is this Adversary called the Satan in Job? Some scholars don't believe he's the same Satan talked about in the New Testament. They argue that Job's accuser is simply a prosecutor in God's heavenly court who is just doing his job. While there's no way to prove it one way or the other, I think they're wrong. My personal hunch is that Job's accuser is indeed the devil. Adolf Hitler was often called "the Führer," signifying both a title and a function, but leaving no doubt as to who, exactly, was being spoken about.

Aside from his brief and contested mention in 1 Chronicles 21:1, the uppercase Satan appears only one other time in the Old Testament, again playing the role of the courtly accuser/tester. Let's turn to Zechariah 3:1–5.

> Then he [the angel of the Lord, understood by man to be the pre-incarnate Christ] showed me [Zechariah] Joshua the high priest [representing the people of God] standing before the angel of the Lord, and [the Adversary] standing at his right hand to accuse him. And the Lord said to [the Adversary], "The Lord rebuke you, O [the Adversary]! The Lord who has chosen Jerusalem rebuke you! Is not this a brand plucked from the fire?" Now Joshua was standing before the angel, clothed with filthy garments. And the angel said to those who were standing before him, "Remove the filthy garments from him." And to him he said, "Behold, I have taken your iniquity away from you, and I will clothe you with pure vestments." And I said, "Let them put a clean turban on his head." So they put a clean turban on his head and clothed him with garments. And the angel of the Lord was standing by.

Notice this time, that we don't even get to hear the Satan's accusation against the poor God-follower in question. Did the Satan dislike Joshua's dirty outfit? Did he think he was doing a shoddy job as high priest? Verse 2 suggests an anti-Jerusalem bent to the accusation. Verse 4 suggests the possibility of a genuine iniquity on the high priest's part. But it doesn't matter, because God has wiped it away.

The devil is our accuser. Jesus is our advocate. He's the defense attorney who makes a case for our righteousness: "Don't you get it, devil? I plucked my disciples from the fires of sin and death and hell. They are perfectly righteous before God because of their faith in me. God, being a God of justice, has no choice but to declare them righteous because I already paid the wages of their sin by dying."

That's it for explicit appearances of capital-S Satan in the Old Testament. The Adversary accuses Job, and then the Adversary accuses Zechariah. The end.

There are other Hebrew *satans* mentioned in the Old Testament:

David calls several of his warriors satans (adversaries) in 2 Samuel 19:22.

Two enemies of David's son King Solomon are called satans (adversaries) in 1 Kings 11:14 and 11:23.

David's enemies are satans (accusers) in Psalm 109:4, which reads, "In return for my love they accuse [*satan*] me." And in verse 6, David asks that a satan (accuser) stand against those enemies.

In 1 Kings 5:4, King Solomon writes to another king that he's finally achieved peace, and there is no satan (adversary) making trouble.

Those who tried to stop Judah and Benjamin from rebuilding the temple in Ezra 4:6 were satans, as they wrote an accusation.

In Numbers 22:32, the angel of the Lord says he has "come out to oppose [*satan*]" a pagan prophet. That's right: Even God's angels can act satanically.

All these folks are satans. They are adversaries. You've had many satans pass through your life. You have been a satan to a great many people. Only God knows how many times I've acted satanically.

In case you're wondering, satan is pronounced saw-tawn. When we accuse others or are adversarial toward them, we're acting sawtawnic.

Things can be satanic without the devil's involvement. China's dictator Xi Jinping's deviousness is Orwellian despite his being born three years after George Orwell's death. Chummy Eton and Oxford British politicians make Churchillian speeches all the time. The hard reality is that the devil may not have even been present in the death camps of Auschwitz and Dachau—he probably was far too busy in Hitler's heart and the pulpits and pews of German churches.

Anyone and anything can be a satan and act satanically, and we have lost all sense of proportion regarding the satanic in our world. The church and media fixate on the occasional report of a "possession" or satanic cult, but ignore that which is evil that adversarially lays waste to generations of people created in the image of God. In case I am not making my point clear enough, let me put it on the record: Pornography is satanic. Racism is satanic. Taking advantage of the poor is satanic. All that is adversarial to the flourishing of creation is satanic.

This is a real brain twister for people like me who grew up in church and assume the devil is lurking on every page of Scripture. Yet, in actual fact, the capital-S Satan appears in just two stories (three at the max) in the whole Old Testament. Think about that for a second. The Old Testament is massive—but out of 39 books, 929 chapters, 23,000+ verses, and 600,000+ words, Satan is mentioned just *twice*.

"Well, hold on!" my former self might say. "What about the garden of Eden?"

What about it? There's no mention of the devil, Satan, or Lucifer in the garden of Eden. The Bible starts with two beautiful hymns that envision the creation of the universe, culminating in the creation of a man (in the original Hebrew Genesis 1 and 2 he's never called capital-A Adam) and a woman the man calls Eve.

Genesis 3 then launches into a poetic narrative about a creepy, possibly legged (Genesis 3:14), talking serpent. The serpent is absolutely satanic, but he's never called Satan. Some Jewish and Muslim traditions believe the serpent was a literal snake, others believe the serpent was a demon, and some modern Christian scholars believe it was another angelic being used to test humans. For reasons we will discuss in the final chapter, it is not at all unreasonable to believe the devil indwelled the Eden serpent; my point is that the text never explicitly says so.

So we conclude our survey of the Old Testament. The capital-S Satan explicitly appears in the Old Testament three times.

Of course, Satan must surely appear far more often in the New Testament.

Or does he?

Satan in the New Testament

The first time Satan definitely appears in the Bible with a capital S and no "the"—the first time he is uncontestedly properly addressed by name without the definite article—is in Matthew 4:10, in words spoken by the man Jesus Christ himself: "Then Jesus said to him, 'Be gone, Satan! For it is written, "You shall worship the Lord your God and him only shall you serve."'" How lovely is that? Jesus is the very first person in all of the Bible to directly address Satan by name, and the first phrase He says to him is "Be gone."

The Greek word *satanas* appears thirty-six times in the New Testament; in twenty-eight of those instances it is preceded by the definite article, as in "the Satan." The Adversary. There are only eight verses without the definite article. Eight capital-S, no-*the* Satanas in the whole New Testament. Most of the mentions of Satan and the Satan are by people talking *about* him and don't actually include him. *Satan* or *the Satan* actually make an appearance on only three occasions.

1. The temptation of Jesus in the wilderness
   (Mark 1 = Matthew 4 = Luke 4).*
2. The tempting/entering of Judas Iscariot
   (Luke 22:3 and John 13:27).
3. When he's hurled from heaven, locked up for a thousand
   years, and released (Revelation 12 and 20).

That's it. Capital-S, no-*the* Satan makes an appearance on just three occasions in the New Testament. Once at the beginning, once in the middle, and once near the end. As my friend theologian Richard John Saunders put it in a recent conversation, "He pops up on the scene at the beginning of the gospels, is firmly trounced by Jesus in the wilderness, and we never hear from him again. It's over before it begins."

I hope you're beginning to see the theme here. The Bible is all about Christ and not even remotely about Satan.

What's our running total? The devil as Lucifer appears zero times. The devil as Satan definitely appears in five-ish scenes. But surely the devil as "The Devil" must appear far more often in the Bible than this.

Right?

---

* Keen Bible hunters have pointed out the Gospel of John might also contain parallels to the three temptations in John 6:26, 31; John 2:18; and John 6:15.

3

DEVIL

"We are each our own devil, and we make this world our hell."

—Oscar Wilde, *The Duchess of Padua*

IF YOU THOUGHT THE NAME LUCIFER was tricky, and Satan was trickier, wait until you see what's up with the devil.

The Greek word for devil is *diabolos*. It means accuser, but there's more bite to it than the Old Testament *adversary*. There's an implied malice, and for the Greeks, a diabolos was a false accuser, a defamer. Secular Greeks called slanderers devils all the time. The devil isn't the only devil in the New Testament. Second Timothy 3:3 says men in the last days will be devils. Titus 2:3 tells older Christian women not to be devils. In 1 Timothy 3:11, one of the qualifications for becoming a deacon is that their wives cannot be devils. Evidently, slander was just as big a problem in the early church as it is in our day.

Diabolos appears just thirty-eight times in the New Testament; twenty-eight of them are preceded by the word *the*. As in, *the* Devil. *The* Accuser. There are only ten verses without the definite article. Just ten capital-D, no-*the* Devils in the whole New Testament. What's most important at present is to note that most of the mentions of Devil and the Devil are by people talking *about* him and don't actually include him. Devil or the Devil actually only makes an appearance on three occasions.

1. There's the temptation of Jesus, which we already covered in our Satan word search.
2. There's the prompting of Judas to betray, which we already covered in our Satan word search.
3. There's the hurling from heaven and being jailed that we already covered in our Satan word search.

Lucifer, Satan, the Satan, Devil, the devil—call him what you will—only definitively appears five times in the entire Bible. He accuses and tests Job, he accuses Joshua, he tests Jesus, he enters Judas, and he is punished for his sins. There are fewer than a hundred total mentions of Satan and the devil in the Bible, a quarter of which are spoken by Jesus. The Bible talks more about donkeys than it does about the devil. The Bible contains more stories about olive oil than about Satan. Satan ranks somewhere between cheese and bread.

As we've seen, Satan is not the only satan, the devil is not the only devil, and if he was a former lucifer, he's certainly not a lucifer, the Lucifer, or Lucifer now.

So a question arises: What in the world should we call him?

New Names

My family is a nickname family. My real name is Jared, but to the fam, I'm Jay. My wife, Michelle, gets called Äiti, Selly, Shell,

Beans, and Berry. Father Gord is Gordo, George, and Papa G; mother Karen is Mama, Sharon, Grammy, and Grandma; sister Ruthann is Rudy to most and Carlita to me; brother Ben is Benner, and so on. Brother-in-law Michael is Mano. Sister-in-law Joanne is Jo. Niece Inez is Nezzy. My father-in-law, Ari, is called Mummi-pappa. My son, Concord (meaning peace and togetherness), gets everything from Conky to Conk-a-donks to Concordito Babysito Señorito. Everyone gets a nickname. You aren't family until we've changed your name.

One thing I adore about the Bible is how frequently people are given a nickname or new name that is infused with meaning.

Abram is called Abraham ("father of many nations").

Sarai is called Sarah ("mother of nations").

Jacob is called Israel ("he struggles with God").

Joseph (of technicolor dreamcoat fame) is called Zaphenath-Paneah.

Moses called his assistant Hoshea ("salvation") Yehoshua ("YHWH is salvation"). We call him Joshua.

Naomi is called Mara.

Daniel is called Belteshazzar.

Hadassah is called Esther.

Simon is called Cephas/Peter, aka Rocky.

James and John are called Boanerges ("sons of thunder").

Thomas is called Didymus ("twin").

John is called Mark.

Tabitha is called Dorcas.

Joseph is called Barnabas ("son of encouragement").

Yet another Joseph, a member of the crime family that arranges Jesus's killing, is called Caiaphas.

Saul is called Paul ("humble").

Evidently, meaning and purpose matter more to God than the earthly name on the long-form birth certificate. Revelation 2:17 suggests God has a purposed name for all Christians: "He who has an ear, let him hear what the Spirit says to the churches. To the one who conquers I will give some of the hidden manna, and I will give him a white stone, with a new name written on the stone that no one knows except the one who receives it."

For eons, the devil has been called the devil, Satan, and Lucifer, but as we've seen, none of these names are likely his *real* proper name, but rather are roles, titles, and activities assigned to him and others, but eventually subsumed by his larger-than-life character.

So what should we call him? Lucifer is definitely off the table. Devil and Satan are far too loaded down with baggage and mental imagery to be useful in helping us gain a clearer image of the foe. Should we resort to the Greek and Hebrew, calling him *diabolos* and *hasatan*? Even those leave us a bit fuzzy unless we remember that diabolos = accuser and satan = adversary, and that the terms are roughly synonymous. I think the most appropriate English name for the devil is the one that strips away the fear and superstition while retaining the roles that describe him—the roles that readers in the original languages would have immediately understood because his names *were* his roles. We'll capitalize both roles to help us remember this is the name of a specific entity. What I've come up with is unwieldy but helpful, and we'll use it for the rest of this book:

We shall call him *Accuser-Adversary*.

It doesn't roll off the tongue, I'll grant you that, and I'm certainly not saying this is a better name for the devil. But it gets across his main task: Accusing believers before God. My goal is simply to give us a name that equates roughly to the effect that the name *satan* would have for Hebrew readers and *diabolos* would have for Greek readers. (And before we get too hung up on the idea of anglicizing the devil's name to make it more understandable to the modern English mind, let's not forget that previous generations did the same thing when they turned the Hebrew Yehoshua ben Yehoseph into the English Jesus of Nazareth.)

Now that we've settled on a new English moniker for the devil, let's see what he looks like.

PART II
APPEARANCE AND ALLIES

4

THE POINTY RED DEVIL

"Listen, child—if you're at a party with a hundred people and one
of them is the devil, he'll be the last one you'd suspect."

—Dean Koontz, *Deeply Odd*

WHAT DOES ACCUSER-ADVERSARY look like? I recently typed "the
devil satan lucifer" into DALL·E 3 and asked artificial intelligence
to generate an image. I didn't include any descriptions whatsoever,
just Accuser-Adversary's three most common names. Here's what
the AI came up with.[1]

As you can see, it contains many of the tropes of the satanic
figure. He has horns and a goatee. He has long claws and fiery
red eyes. His skin is scaly and black. He carries a pitchfork. He
has wings and wears a red cape. He's surrounded by flames. He
looks downright evil.

AI, of course, is only taking its cues from the data available. It
was human beings who told AI what Accuser-Adversary looks like.

There's only one major problem with the various and sundry features of the AI's Accuser-Adversary: Precisely none of them are biblically accurate.

My wife attended the University of Guelph, famous for its rather disfigured cannon. Each night, students paint the cannon with the colors of their home nation, sorority, favorite football team, or what have you, and then guard it until dawn. Every summer, the university sandblasts away hundreds of layers of paint, until they get down to what approximates the form of a long-retired projectile-tossing artillery field piece.

That is unfortunately the best we can hope to accomplish with Accuser-Adversary. Before we can paint an accurate picture of him, we must first strip him down to base metal, however lumpy that may be. Shall we work our way from head to toe?

Horns

By the number of depictions of Accuser-Adversary crowned with horns, one wonders if the devil isn't half goat. The Roman half-goat god Pan sported a giant erection, and ancient gods and goddesses were often topped with horns as a sign of fertility, sexuality, and untamable animalistic wildness. (It's perhaps an obscure source of the slang term *horny*. If you're experiencing erectile dysfunction, horny goat weed is said to help.) But just because Dionysus, Isis, and Baal are frequently depicted with horns doesn't automatically mean Accuser-Adversary has horns. We are people of the book, and if we don't see it in the Word of God, we don't assume he looks like the various demons, devils, and demigods that littered the ancient landscape.

The idea that Accuser-Adversary has horns might spring from several places in the Bible. The first is a vision by the prophet Daniel, in which he sees four beasts, one of which has ten horns (Daniel 7:7). But Daniel 7:24 makes it clear: These beasts and these horns represent real, actual, human kingdoms and kings, not

Accuser-Adversary. John has a similar vision in Revelation 13:1, except this time it's one beast with seven heads and ten horns. But Revelation 13:2 makes it clear that while the beast is *empowered* by Accuser-Adversary, it's not actually Accuser-Adversary himself. Another beast (this time with two horns) appears a few verses later, but again, this one is only *like* Accuser-Adversary (Revelation 13:11). This might mean Accuser-Adversary actually does have horns, but the Bible never definitively says so. Another seven-headed, ten-horned beast crops up in Revelation 17:3, but Revelation 17:12 says the ten horns represent ten future kings.

Fiery Red Eyes

We've all heard of the evil eye—I experienced it in the *Lord of the Rings* and from my grandmother when I started a fire in her microwave—and it no doubt signifies anger and rage. One source for this red-pupil myth might be the *Codex Gigas*, aka "the Devil's Bible." As the story goes, a monk named Herman the Recluse broke his vows and was slated to be walled up alive and starved to death, so he promised his abbot he would create a Bible in a single night that would bring fame to the monastery forever. By midnight it became abundantly clear that he would not finish by sunrise—modern experts from National Geographic estimate it would take at least twenty years to create such a colossal work of art—so he sold the devil his soul in exchange for completing the book. Herman finished in time and included a drawing of the devil as thanks. The thirteenth-century Bohemian work is the largest surviving illuminated medieval manuscript in the world, weighing 165 pounds, but it's jam-packed with author-added paganism and folklore, and even though Herman's devil has red eyes, it doesn't mean we should believe Accuser-Adversary actually does.

Revelation 19:12 (NIV) is mistakenly attributed to Accuser-Adversary by some. "His eyes are like blazing fire, and on his head are many crowns." There are multiple mentions of fiery eyes in the Bible, but they're never attributed to Accuser-Adversary. Quite the opposite: All mentions of eyes blazing with holy fire belong to God and Jesus alone (Daniel 10:6; Revelation 1:14; Revelation 2:18; Revelation 19:12).

Mustache and/or Goatee

Does anything except perhaps baldness elicit such a cacophonous response to the male visage as facial hair? Some women will not kiss their man if he has so much as a bent whisker on his lip, while others swear divorce and/or murder should their bearded hubbies dare put razor to cheek.

Accuser-Adversary is rarely, if ever, depicted as clean-shaven, nor does he appear with a Santa-like beard. Why is he never seen with a chin strap, muttonchops, or a Fu Manchu? Where is the old Dutch, the French fork, or the soul patch? Considering he's been hanging around humans for thousands of years, Accuser-Adversary has stayed remarkably consistent with his facial hair. The mustache is either a pencil, copstach standard, or a handlebar, and the goatee is invariably a petit or an anchor.

The Bible is full of facial hair—I literally wrote an entire book about it—but as with Accuser-Adversary's supposedly fiery eyes, there's no biblical description of his chin, cheeks, or upper lip. As with the horns, Pan seems a more than likely inspiration. He looks not unlike Narnia's Mr. Tumnas, the faun with his pointy goatee. The post-Constantine Catholics were all too happy to subsume myth and integrate culture to spread the gospel, and by the time the medieval and Renaissance painters got involved, the Pan-devil's facial hair was waxed in stone. Mustaches were wildly popular for centuries (think anywhere from Robin Hood to the Three Musketeers) both with the rich and the poor. Accordingly, the poor assigning the devil the same facial hair as the wicked Prince John seemed apt, as did the rich assigning the devil the same facial hair as the sniveling street paupers of Paris and London and Rome. All of this is exactly what Accuser-Adversary loves, of course—the satanic demonization of those we dislike. Our own times have further cemented Accuser-Adversary's follicle figure, thanks to the mustaches of Hitler, Stalin, Hussein, and Pinochet.

Fiery Sulfur Breath

Various folks in the Bible have visions of Accuser-Adversary in which he appears as a dragon, but not one account explicitly says he breathes fire and brimstone and reeks of eggy sulfur. Perhaps this is projection from the roaring Mesopotamian god Huwawa who shot fire from his mouth? Perhaps there's a lingering cultural memory of the Greek monster Typhon, the evil enemy of Zeus with his hundred snake heads and fiery breath? How about Vulcan, the Roman god of fire and volcanoes?

God rains down sulfur and fire on Sodom and Gomorrah in Genesis 19:24, and Revelation 20:10 predicts Accuser-Adversary will be hurled into a lake of fire and sulfur at the end of days, but neither has anything to do with the devil's mouth. Job 41:19–21 describes a being that might fit the bill: "Out of his mouth go flaming torches; sparks of fire leap forth. Out of his nostrils comes forth smoke, as from a boiling pot and burning rushes. His breath kindles coals, and a flame comes forth from his mouth." But if you look at the context and other passages like Psalm 104:26, the being in question seems to be some sort of real, ancient, prehistoric, sea-frolicking beast (Job 41:1). This "Leviathan" might very well be a metaphor for Accuser-Adversary (Isaiah 27:1), but the Bible never says so.

In a real twist on the tropes, we do have one definitive substance that rushes from Accuser-Adversary's mouth, and it isn't fire. Revelation 12:15–16 says that he spews *water*.

Cape and Tights

We won't belabor this one for more than a moment, aside from noting that while the vast majority of people don't believe Accuser-Adversary actually wears a cape and tights, subconsciously, many of us seldom picture him any other way. Cloaks and capes definitely make an appearance in the Bible. (See Genesis 39:12; 1 Kings 19:13; Acts 12:8, and nearly three dozen other appearances. My favorite is a touchingly human mention in 2 Timothy 4:13, where Paul asks his friend to bring a cloak he left behind in Troas.) But there's no reference to Accuser-Adversary in such garb.

A possible source for the popular cape-and-tights motif is Charles Gounod's 1859 five-act opera, first performed at the Théâtre Lyrique in Paris and loosely based on Goethe's *Faust*. The demon (not devil) character, Mephistopheles, was costumed in Renaissance-era dress that included a cape and tights, called hose. The opera was a smash hit and went viral, so to speak, with translated performances all over Europe and America. That's right: Millions of us today picture the devil in a cape and tights because a Frenchman took a German's story about a demon and sent him to England and America dressed as an Italian.

Wings

Wings are mentioned plenty in the Bible (117 occurrences by my count). Ezekiel 1:6 mentions four creatures (cherubim), each with four wings. Isaiah 6:2 reports a vision of seraphim, each with six wings. Revelation 4:8 envisions four living creatures each with six wings, possibly seraphim but never explicitly called such. Earthly riches disappear in flight (Proverbs 23:4–5). Ezekiel described the Babylonian king Nebuchadnezzar as approximating a peacock in Ezekiel 17:3. David constantly longs for the shelter of the shadow of God's wings (Psalm 17:8; Psalm 36:7; Psalm 57:1; Psalm 61:4; Psalm 63:7). In Psalm 18:10 and 2 Samuel 22:11, David envisions

God mounting a cherub and flying "on the wings of the wind." Boaz, an ancestor of Jesus, also envisions YHWH having wings (Ruth 2:12). Revelation 9:7–10 describes a sort of metallic, winged, locust-and-horse-shaped soldier with a human face—if this describes real physical beings, for my money it's a description of autonomous robot soldiers. But none of the 117 mentions of wings are explicitly connected to Accuser-Adversary.

And then there's Lilith. It sounds like the lovely name of your next-door neighbor's grandmother, but Lilith was a winged Babylonian female demon, a sort of she-vampire, who became (in some Jewish traditions) the first wife of Adam before leaving him to spawn all demons to follow. The serpent in the garden? That's Lilith, so we're told by thirteenth-century Kabbalists. Most Bible translations never mention Lilith by name, but a few do, including the Amplified and the New Revised Standard Versions, and at least four translate the Hebrew *lîlît* (owl or nocturnal animal) in Isaiah 34:14 as a night monster. Still, Lilith isn't equated with Accuser-Adversary, so we can't cut and paste her wings.

If there is a biblical source for the idea of a winged Accuser-Adversary, it could be in reference to the possible dark force behind the kings of Tyre and Babylon (Ezekiel 28:11–19 and Isaiah 14:12–15). John in Revelation 12:3–9 describes Accuser-Adversary as a seven-headed, ten-horned dragon reminiscent of the Canaanite god Labbu and the Greek hydra. The seven heads represent seven kings (Revelation 17:9–10) and the ten horns represent ten future kings (Revelation 17:12–13), but there's no mention of wings here either.

Accuser-Adversary's bat wings first appear around the twelfth century, as artists stripped the devil of his angelic feathers for a more leathery sheen. We need to blame Dante Alighieri for the enduring popularity of a winged Accuser-Adversary. His *Inferno* describes "Lucifer" as having six bat-like, featherless wings, suggesting he sourced his Accuser-Adversary less from Scripture and more from ancient Babylonian myth.

Pitchfork

This is a really strange one. Accuser-Adversary is constantly depicted as carrying a pitchfork, a two-pointed bident, or a trident, with absolutely zero biblical grounding. Isaiah 30:24 mentions a shovel and fork, but only as farming instruments. Job 41:1–2 mentions some sort of pronged hook, but only for spearing massive sea beasts. Meanwhile, the Canaanite god Baal often hefts a spear or thunderbolt. The Greek god Hermes holds a snake-wrapped caduceus staff. The Roman god of war, Mars, wields a spear, and the Roman god of the underworld, Pluto, wields a two-pronged spear. The Hindu god Shiva had a trident, as did one of the twelve Olympians, Poseidon. It appears Accuser-Adversary's trident motif is entirely secular.

Red or Black Skin

Only one person is described in the Bible as having red skin: Jacob's twin brother, Esau, in Genesis 25:25. Where did the conception of a red devil come from? One possible source is Egypt, a civilization already 3,000 years old by the advent of Christ. A god named Set or Seth emerged as the Egyptian personification of evil. He had either red skin or white skin and red hair, and he dwelled in a red land called Dšrt in Egyptian, from which we get the word *desert*. Set occasionally appears as a serpent, and Seth's jealousy and murder of his brother Osiris bears a striking resemblance to the Cain and Abel story. That said, Revelation 12:3 describes Accuser-Adversary as "a great red dragon," symbolizing the bloodthirsty violence of the Roman Empire. Rome's color of choice was red, thanks to its association to Mars, their god of war, and it adorned everything from army standards to soldier cloaks to senatorial robes. When Roman generals were awarded triumphs for victories in battle, they were slathered head to toe in red paint. Kings and cardinals continue to sport red to this very day, which for many strengthens the red devil association.

The other option for Accuser-Adversary's skin tone is black, in this case symbolizing darkness, evil, and death. In Athanasius's report of Saint Anthony's valiant efforts to battle Accuser-Adversary, he describes the enemy: "Finally, the dragon, seeing that he could not overthrow Anthony, was seized by rage. He appeared to Anthony as he is in reality, that is, in the form of a black child."[2]

If Accuser-Adversary isn't a black boy, he's sometimes depicted as a black cat. As the Parisian bishop Guillaume d'Auvergne wrote in the early thirteenth century, Lucifer is permitted "to appear to his worshippers and adorers in the form of a black cat or a toad and to demand kisses from them; whether as a cat, abominably, under the tail; or as a toad, horribly, on the mouth."[3]

We don't have a single artistic impression of Accuser-Adversary prior to the sixth century. His earliest known possible depiction is a mosaic in the Basilica of Sant'Apollinare Nuovo in Ravenna, Italy. He stands behind Jesus on Christ's left, with some goats in front of him, a reference to the parable of the sheep and the goats in Matthew 25:31–46. If the artist is trying to depict the Accuser-Adversary, he makes him look like any other stereotypical angel—wings, halo, Greek toga and sash—except, instead of being white or black, this angel is blue.

Tail

Tails appear thirteen to sixteen times in the Bible, depending on your translation, but it appears the forked tail is yet another Egyptian hand-me-down, this time from their god Anpu, or Anubis. This deity is half man, half beast, with horns and tail. Does the forked tail possibly represent the lash of slavery? Accuser-Adversary's tail was pinned on him by his connection to Revelation 12:4, where the dragon's tail "swept down a third of the stars of heaven and cast them to the earth."

Cloven Hooves

There are twenty-one hooves in the Bible, again depending on your translation. (Or is that twenty-one sets of hooves, for eighty-four hooves in total?) Some animals with cloven hooves that didn't chew the cud were considered unclean under the law of Moses (Leviticus 11:4), but Accuser-Adversary's uncleanness before God doesn't curse him with split feet. It's no stretch to think that some of the images we have of the devil today are holdovers from the Greek and Roman god Pan. Like most satyrs and fauns, Pan had horns and a goatee and hooves for feet. This hairy half-man half-goat was the god of nature and music and fertility, lustful and chaotic, making him a potent symbol of temptation and sin.

This brings us to Matthew 25:31–33. "When the Son of Man comes in his glory, and all the angels with him, then he will sit on his glorious throne. Before him will be gathered all the nations, and he will separate people one from another as a shepherd separates the sheep from the goats. And he will place the sheep on his right, but the goats on the left." Sheep good, goats bad. Jesus is the lamb of God, therefore, the devil must be Pan the goat god. If Accuser-Adversary is the former cherub of Ezekiel 28:14, he may very well have had hooves, considering Ezekiel 1:7 describes cherubim as having feet like those of a cow.

Accuser-Adversary's foot shape was "confirmed" in Devon, England, in February 1855 when, after a heavy snowfall, the "Devil's Footprints" were seen for forty-plus miles. The story spiraled to such dizzying heights that by the time it reached the Australian newspaper *Bell's Life in Sydney* come springtime, the footprints had traveled over houses, walls, gardens, and courtyards. Later theories suggested the tracks were made by a donkey, a pony, a hopping mouse, a badger, a kangaroo, and the shackles of a runaway hot-air balloon.

There ends our survey of the devil's so-called appearance. Various bits and bobs reached international prominence through the fictitious writings of novelists, including Dante at the start of the Renaissance, Milton during the English Civil War, and Goethe during the late Enlightenment. Many of their descriptions have been cemented into popular culture by advertisers, from Underwood Deviled Ham Spread to Match.com's "The Devil Met His Match" campaign. Accuser-Adversary plays extremely well with audiences, and has appeared in commercials for Kia, Axe, M&Ms, Snickers, Pepsi, Little Caesars, Mercedes-Benz, Doritos, Skittles, and hundreds more. Even the hit Christian TV show *The Chosen* created nine comedic video ads featuring a devil character who tries to prevent Christians from watching the show about Jesus and His disciples. Angel Studios then brilliantly defaced forty-eight of their own *The Chosen* billboards with spray paint that directed people to TheChosenIsNotGood.com.

In Hollywood as well, Accuser-Adversary is boffo at the box office. *The Exorcist, The Conjuring, Rosemary's Baby, The Omen, The Exorcism of Emily Rose,* the list goes on and on. *The Devil Wears Prada* made $326 million in cinemas alone. My favorite depiction of Accuser-Adversary is the 1997 film *The Devil's Advocate,* in which Al Pacino plays a more-corrupt-than-usual lawyer who turns out to be (spoiler alert) the devil himself.

In review, our current image of Accuser-Adversary is a mishmash of Egyptian gods, Canaanite deities, Greek monsters and members of the Roman pantheon, a dash of Middle Ages Italian creativity and nineteenth-century French operatics, solidified by Hollywood movie studios and dozens of major American brands. In other words, our image of Accuser-Adversary is thoroughly unbiblical.

Now that we've torn up the picture of what he *doesn't* look like, let's see if we can dig through the biblical photo album and make an approximate collage.

The New (Original) Image

When God created the being we now call the devil, he was good. He was beautiful, did meaningful and God-glorifying work, and lived as a faithful servant of the Most High. God did not create the devil we know today any more than a loving mother creates a son who grows up to become a mass murderer or child rapist. God created a beautiful being of light and truth and goodness, but then Accuser-Adversary chose rebellion.

What does the devil actually look like? The answer, quite frustratingly, is, it depends. Being a spirit, the devil doesn't have a physical body (except when he enters non-Christian bodies like demons do), so we can rule out any permanent features like toenails and nipples and wisdom teeth. Being made by God and not born of womankind, he joins Adam in not having a belly button.

To glean an approximation of the devil's appearance, it's helpful to start with this question: What is the devil? Is the devil simply a fallen angel, or is he in a special category of his own? The devil is never called a fallen angel in Scripture. In fact, it was more than a hundred years after the death of Christ—and more than a millennia after Accuser-Adversary's first mention in Job—that writers connected the devil to a passage in Isaiah about the king of Babylon (Isaiah 14:12). It was Origen who popularized the connection with Luke 10:18, and a new satanology was off to the races.

Accuser-Adversary is never explicitly called an angel, cherubim, or seraphim in the Bible, but we have good reason to believe he was something of that order. Even if he wasn't, Paul sets us straight in 2 Corinthians 11:13–15. "For such men are false apostles, deceitful workmen, disguising themselves as apostles of Christ. And no wonder, for even Satan disguises himself as an angel of light. So it is no surprise if his servants, also, disguise themselves as servants of righteousness."

There we have it: Even if Accuser-Adversary wasn't originally an angel, which he probably was, he now disguises himself as an angel of light. He presents like a radiant messenger. A lucifer. We're surrounded by all sorts of shiny messengers these days, and it's hard to discern who represents the true light and who's just disguising the darkness: Fashion pastors preaching moral thera-peutic deism. Televangelists schilling for donations in exchange for magic healing cloths. Christian radio money gurus helping you get rich by exploiting the poor.

Let's presume for the moment that Accuser-Adversary was or is an angel, or at the very least disguises himself as one. On that basis, we can get a good idea of his possible appearance.

In Matthew 28:2–3, an angel has the appearance of lightning and his clothing is as white as snow.

In Isaiah 6:2, seraphim have six wings, and "with two he covered his face, and with two he covered his feet, and with two he flew."

Ezekiel 10:8 notes "The cherubim appeared to have the form of a human hand under their wings."

An angel in Revelation 10:1–2 appears "wrapped in a cloud, with a rainbow over his head, and his face was like the sun, and his legs like pillars of fire."

This Daniel 10:6 description of a heavenly being is particularly evocative: "His body was like beryl, his face like the appearance of lightning, his eyes like flaming torches, his arms and legs like the gleam of burnished bronze, and the sound of his words like the sound of a multitude."

Ezekiel 1:5–14 and Revelation 4:6–8 paint cinematic-universe-worthy pictures. Psalm 104:4 suggests angels can appear as wind or fire. In Revelation 1:20, angels are represented as stars. According to Luke 20:36, angels live forever. Clearly, these texts are deeply symbolic, and entire libraries have been written about angels.

I want to camp for a moment on Ezekiel 28:11–19, as it's an important passage with a possible double meaning at play—a text that denounces a real earthly king but then gets eerily devilish. The king in the crosshairs this time is Ithobaal III, the Baal-worshiping king of Tyre. The historical political context in brief: The uber-wealthy Tyrian kings had long been trading partners of Israel, most notably when Hiram I helped Solomon build the temple (1 Kings 5:1–18). Not that it was all roses—it was the Tyrians who gave Israel the ultra-wicked queen Jezebel and at one point they even sold Jewish children as sex slaves (Joel 3:3–7).

The straw that broke the camel's back occurred when the Babylonian king Nebuchadnezzar besieged Jerusalem in 589 BC. Ithobaal III didn't come to Israel's aid. Quite the opposite. In Ezekiel 26:2, the prophet reports the glee with which Tyrians beheld the sack of Jerusalem: "Aha, the gate of the peoples is broken; it has swung open to me. I shall be replenished, now that she is laid waste." Thus, Ezekiel's holy tirade predicting Tyre's destruction. Sure enough, after Jerusalem fell in 587/586 BC, Nebuchadnezzar immediately turned his sights on Tyre, besieging it for thirteen years until it fell in 573 BC.

Unlike the Isaiah 14 passage about the king of Babylon, which lists a bunch of definitely earthly king descriptions before opening the door to the possibility of a secondary spiritual target, Ezekiel writes a quick introduction and immediately goes otherworldly. The text is so wild that I include it here in full:

> Moreover, the word of the Lord came to me: "Son of man, raise a lamentation over the king of Tyre, and say to him, Thus says the Lord GOD:
>
> "You were the signet of perfection,
>   full of wisdom and perfect in beauty.
> You were in Eden, the garden of God;
>   every precious stone was your covering,
> sardius, topaz, and diamond,
>   beryl, onyx, and jasper,
> sapphire, emerald, and carbuncle;
>   and crafted in gold were your settings
>   and your engravings.
> On the day that you were created
>   they were prepared.
> You were an anointed guardian cherub.
>   I placed you; you were on the holy mountain of God;
>   in the midst of the stones of fire you walked.

You were blameless in your ways
    from the day you were created,
    till unrighteousness was found in you.
In the abundance of your trade
    you were filled with violence in your midst, and you
        sinned;
so I cast you as a profane thing from the mountain of
    God,
    and I destroyed you, O guardian cherub,
    from the midst of the stones of fire.
Your heart was proud because of your beauty;
    you corrupted your wisdom for the sake of your
        splendor.
I cast you to the ground;
    I exposed you before kings,
    to feast their eyes on you.
By the multitude of your iniquities,
    in the unrighteousness of your trade
    you profaned your sanctuaries;
so I brought fire out from your midst;
    it consumed you,
and I turned you to ashes on the earth
    in the sight of all who saw you.
All who know you among the peoples
    are appalled at you;
you have come to a dreadful end
    and shall be no more forever."

Ezekiel 28:11–19

What in the world?

King Ithobaal III of Tyre was not the epitome of perfection. He wasn't in Eden. He definitely wasn't a guardian angel. Blameless? No. Fire-walker? No. Wearing more jewels than Liberace? Maybe.

As with the Isaiah 14 passage about the king of Babylon, Origen believed this lamentation was about the spiritual force behind the king of Tyre. From his perspective, Ezekiel is reminding the king of Tyre about the fate of all those who follow Accuser-Adversary's path. This time, Gregory the Great agreed with Origen, as did Tertullian, Cyprian, Jerome, and Augustine. It's entirely possible that Ezekiel just pulled these images out of thin air as a poetic critique of Ithobaal's lofty pride, but I strongly doubt it. Here's why. Ezekiel 28 is split into two sections: a word for the prince of Tyre, and a lamentation over the king of Tyre. The first half, verses 1–10, seems very much to describe the actions of the real man—prideful, sea-adjacent, wealthy due to trade, ruthless in battle—but then the second half is chock full of heavenly imagery. My hunch? The earthly king Ithobaal III is reduced by YHWH and Ezekiel to mere prince in the passage, while Accuser-Adversary is the true king of Tyre. If this is true, then Ezekiel 28 is about both.

Despite the varying modern opinions and the lack of explicit connection in Scripture, let's presume Accuser-Adversary is the truest target of Ezekiel 28. If so, we learn a lot about him, whether the visuals are symbolic or not. The first thing to point out is that he was a cherub. Cherubim were worshipers, leading some theologians to speculate that the devil was originally the head of heaven's worship team. The priestly music pastor, so to speak. Ezekiel 28:13–14 also seems to support the idea of Accuser-Adversary previously being a musical archangel in God's presence, though more recent translations sometimes footnote the uncertainness of the original Hebrew meaning of the words in verse 13 translated in earlier versions as "timbrels" and "pipes" instead of the "settings" and "engravings" we read here in the ESV.

But unrighteousness was found in him. What was it that tripped him up? "Your heart was proud because of your beauty." Imagine that. Imagine being created and adorned by God himself, only to take pride in your appearance as if you had anything to do with it. This is something we've never done, of course. ☺ I've never even once been the slightest bit puffed up by a book launch, a film premiere, a successful TV interview, an hourlong book signing, or growing my first chest hair in high school. We never let social media likes or follows go to our head. Surely no Christian has ever become prideful at "our" skills and talents and looks and achievements and drive and motivation and our millions of other unearned privileges. Like you and me, Accuser-Adversary forgot that everything was a gift from God and stopped acting accordingly. Accuser-Adversary rejected God's right-way-of-livingness. Until that moment, he was perfect in all his ways, beautiful, blinged in jewelry, a guardian cherub, a fire-walker.

Not the stereotypical red-scaled, horn-headed, pointy-goateed, pitchfork-wielding, cape-wearing devil we picture, is it? But after that moment of choosing rebellion he could only *disguise* himself as an angel of light.

So there we have it.

The old (formalized Christendom) image: "Lucifer" the satanic devil has horns, fiery red eyes, a mustache or goatee, fiery sulfur breath, a cape and tights, bat wings, a pitchfork or trident, red or black skin, a forked tail, and cloven hooves.

The new (original) image: Whatever his true appearance is now, Accuser-Adversary disguises himself as a gorgeous, glorious, radiant, awesome, awe-inspiring angel of light.

It's important that we see Accuser-Adversary as he presents himself—not usually repulsive, terrifying, or revolting—or we're far more likely to fall for his tricks. As Tucker Max put it in his memoir, "The devil doesn't come dressed in a red cape and pointy horns. He comes as everything you've ever wished for."[4]

But Is He Real?

Is Accuser-Adversary a real individual being, or is he just a representation of sin and evil and the symbol of our collective rebellion against God? You can certainly read Scripture in the latter way. After all, he makes only five-ish appearances in the Bible, all of which might not have physically happened. Let's play unreal-devil's advocate: Accuser-Adversary appears in the possibly allegorical story of Job, then in Zechariah's vision, then goes radio silent until his possibly-a-spiritual-vision testing of Jesus in the wilderness. After his entering of Judas (surely in spirit form), he doesn't show up again until Revelation, but even there, there's a huge amount of speculation about how much of this is in the future and how much is in reference to the Roman Empire. Maybe Accuser-Adversary is also the Eden snake, but who's to say the two Genesis creation hymns—or at least the serpent in them— aren't allegorical?

Perhaps he's both, but the fact that Jesus directly addresses him suggests Accuser-Adversary is more than a self-projection, that he is an actual persona and specific enemy of God and humanity. Jesus certainly seems to think he's a real being, and as we'll see, sin and rebellion still will exist without Accuser-Adversary. Charles Baudelaire wrote, "The Devil's finest trick is to persuade you that he does not exist!"[5]

That said, it appears God denies this being one of the things he needs to accomplish its purposes—real personhood. Accuser-Adversary has a personality, but he isn't a person. God has reduced him to his roles, but God hasn't made him personal.

There's a bit of a Pascal's wager at play here. If Accuser-Adversary is just a metaphor, then believing he's also a real being does no harm. But if Accuser-Adversary is a real being and we deny his existence, we're opening ourselves up to a world of unnecessary risk and attack. There's simply no upside to ruling out the possibility of his actual existence. Fulton Sheen wrote in *Life of Christ*,

> Very few people believe in the devil these days, which suits the devil very well. He is always helping to circulate the news of his own death. The essence of God is existence, and He defines Himself as: "I am Who am." The essence of the devil is the lie, and he defines himself as: "I am who I am not." Satan has very little trouble with those who do not believe in him; they are already on his side.[6]

It is vital to Accuser-Adversary that you do not believe in a real spiritual realm. In C. S. Lewis's *The Screwtape Letters*, the demon Screwtape warns his nephew-trainee Wormwood, "When they believe in us, we cannot make them materialists and sceptics."[7]

Materialism is the term for the denial of a spiritual realm. Materialism assumes reality is composed solely of matter and energy. Why would one assume that? We can't empirically prove love, faith, hope, grace, hate, or the soul, so why leap to the conclusion that the material is all there is? Why not at the very least leave the door open to possibility? Or is there more at work here? Is there—dare I say—a spirit that shuts the door to the possibility of a spiritual dimension beyond the physical?

One of the best arguments in favor of a maker is that something rather than nothing exists. It's deceptively simple, which is why most people ignore it. Why does stuff exist instead of not exist? The very existence of things tips the scales slightly in favor of a something maker.

I don't like the sort of closed-minded atheist thinking that can't even admit the *possibility* of the supernatural beyond the natural and the eternal beyond the temporal. It is the sort of extremist thinking that signals a serious God complex. How can someone who cannot even prove their memories or their own existence possibly be trustworthy about so grand a claim as God's status? We are not know-nothings, but we are not know-it-alls. Indeed, we are likely far nearer the former than the latter. "I think. I hope. I believe. I have faith. I am convinced. . . ." These are the statements of reasonable minds. To rule out mere possibility is to be a fundamentalist. The last thing we need in this world is more know-it-all arrogance. This is what makes today's materialist mindset so covertly dangerous—it is callous in the extreme, cold, hard, calculating, narrow-minded, hard-headed, hard-hearted, closed off from those with differing perspectives, exclusionary. In other words, materialism is everything that its proponents claim to hate.

Materialists don't even believe in the existence of evil. In the materialist metaverse, evil is not a hardware problem, but just a temporary software systems glitch that can be fixed with a few better lines of coding. How many demagogues have promised utopia just around the corner if only we improve education, the economic system, or the political order? To be sure, some economic systems spread well-being more widely than others. Wisdom is proven right by what it produces (Matthew 11:19; Luke 7:35). Some political systems spread power more widely than others. Some education systems spread knowledge and wisdom more widely than others. We can and should use all three tools to improve life for the weak and poor, but no physical system can change the spiritual heart.

Materialism—the idea that matter matters more than people—leads to a dangerous slavery as matter becomes the god. A few million incinerated Jews don't really matter—they were just atoms, after all. An aboriginal nation's water source doesn't matter nearly as much as corporate profits for Big Oil shareholders. Matter cannot have ultimacy. It makes people into objects, mere things instead of eternal beings created in the image of God. A thing can then be treated as a tool. A thing can be treated as capital. A thing can be used. A thing can be mistreated. A thing can be controlled. A thing can be consumed. A thing can be ignored and abandoned. A thing can be destroyed. Much of the world has now entered an age of hyper-individualist materialist consumerism. No wonder the West is collapsing.

When we decide to deny the spiritual God and make our own material meaning, we knowingly lie to ourselves, and in doing so open the door for untold pathologies including the inability to discern the countless lies of others. As Dan Allender is quoted in *Between Heaven and the Real World* by Steven Curtis Chapman, "Satan is screaming lies over us all day long. And God whispers the truth in a still, small voice. So often the voice we listen to most is the one we hear loudest."[8]

The materialist worldview is literally life-threatening. This is the same satanic mindset that drove the resurrection-denying Sadducee high priest Annas Ben Sethi to engineer the assassination of Jesus after Christ disrupted his economic exploitation of the Israelite Passover crowds. (See my book *A God Named Josh* for the whole sordid affair.) If this life is really all that there is, then it is *rational* to amass as much power and wealth as feasibly possible.

It's vital we know what Accuser-Adversary looks like—in both a material and spiritual sense—so we can more easily spot him at work in the world around us. He rarely appears as the water-spewing dragon. Fear is not nearly as powerful as seduction.

If you want to be keenly aware of the satanic, **stay on the lookout for the material without the spiritual**: beauty without humility, riches without contribution, knowledge without wisdom, action without mission, justice without mercy, receiving without giving, tolerance without discernment, rights without foundation, sex without commitment, communication without meaning, enjoyment without gratitude, distraction without purpose, power without stewardship, and being without love. All that glitters is not gold.

5

IN CAHOOTS WITH THE DEVIL

"'Come,' he said, 'come, we must see and act. Devils or no devils, or all the devils at once, it matters not; we fight him all the same.'"

—Bram Stoker, *Dracula*

WE WON'T SPEND MUCH TIME on demons because this is a book about Accuser-Adversary, but here's the rest of the story of my father Gord's phone call with a demon. Mike (name changed to protect his identity) called Gord because something or someone had recently started speaking through him and Mike was reasonably freaked out about it. The moment Gord started sharing the gospel with Mike, his voice morphed into that of a decidedly otherworldly old-timey crackling radio. Every hair on my father's body stood at attention. "Tell me your name," Gord said. "My name is Legion." It was probably a lie. They went back and forth for a minute until the demon started cursing and swearing so loudly that Gord had to hold the phone away from his head.

"Face your future," Gord said. "You're going to spend eternity in hell with the devil." At that point, the demon started screaming in Cantonese. My father was having none of it. "In the name of Jesus I command you to be silent." The demon replied, "You have one minute, Pastor." Mike's sobbing voice came back on the line. He was scared and upset. He had no idea where it had come from or how he'd let it in. My dad opened his Bible to Ephesians 6 and explained that if Mike was a true believer and follower of Jesus, he could appeal to the armor of God. The demon came back almost exactly a minute later. Dad silenced it before it got started. "I will only speak with Mike."

My father later learned Mike's girlfriend had been raised in a home with an abusive alcoholic father. The violence was so horrific that during one of his work trips, the mother had hired a carpenter to install a secret room under the kitchen floor. When the father came home with his friends, Mike's girlfriend would hide in the hole with her imaginary friend. She had carried the friend her whole life, and had evidently passed it to or shared it with Mike. The first time Mike manifested, he disclosed details he'd never been told—he named every guy his girlfriend had ever slept with from her teen years up to her forties.

There are a number of words for demons in the Bible, including demons, devils, evil spirits, and unclean spirits. The phrase *evil spirit* or *evil spirits* appears twenty-four times in the ESV Bible, including some occurrences in the Old Testament, where evil spirits are sent by God to torment or punish people who disobey him. The phrase *unclean spirit* or *unclean spirits* appears 22 times in the ESV Bible. Mark 5:2–18 suggests demons and unclean spirits can be one and the same.

The Jewish Talmud has much to say about demons—far too much. Some of the unmissable gems include the assertion that demons were created at twilight before the first Sabbath (Pesachim 54a), are known to haunt bathrooms (Berakhot 62b) and drain gutters (Chullin 105b), and are ready at all times to destroy the fool who returns a cup of asparagus wine to anyone besides the person who gave it to him (Berakhot 51a). For those wondering, various preventions for bathroom demons include pooping while facing only north or south, wiping with your left hand instead of your right hand, having a goat accompany you, or rattling a nut in a copper vessel.

Jewish demons possess impressive powers, including the ability to turn people's faces backward (Baba Mezi'a 86a) and make cedar trees swallow them whole (Sanhedrin 101a). The king of the demons is not Accuser-Adversary but a fellow named Ashmedai, who torments anyone who imbibes alcohol in pairs (Pesahim 110a). There are plenty of demons in this schema—a thousand at every person's left and ten thousand at every person's right, if we believe Berakhot 6a. Accuser-Adversary himself is barely mentioned in the Talmud and is little more than a demon with the ability to turn himself into a bird or a deer.

Even if all this seems a bit farfetched, please don't be tempted to make fun of the Talmud's ancient writers—according to Gittin 57a, anyone who makes fun of sages will be boiled in excrement.

Despite the Talmud's clear obsession (delight?) in demonry, my favorite demon tale comes to us from the quill of Pope Gregory the Great. In his *Dialogues*, he relays the story of a hungry nun who devours a garden lettuce without making the sign of the cross and accidentally swallows a demon. When the exorcist evicts the evil creature, the demon complains, "What have I done? I was sitting there upon the lettice [sic], and she came and did eat me."[1] Gregory's greatly overactive imagination also led him to publish and popularize an official list of seven deadly sins, even though Romans 6:23 makes it quite clear that *all* sin is deadly.

Christians shouldn't get too hung up on demons. When the ancient Greeks used the word *daimōn*, they were talking about all sorts of things, including gods, spirits, fortune, fate, genius, inspiration, even their own conscience. It was between the writing of the Old and New Testaments, when Jews came into contact with Greek culture, that the word *daimōnion* was adopted by Greek-speaking Jews to describe sinister spirits.

The proper word for demons, *daimōnes*, appears only *once* in the Greek New Testament. It's in Matthew 8:31 within the story of Jesus casting a legion of demons into a herd of pigs. All other references to "demons" in the New Testament—all sixty-three of them—are references to evil spirits (*daimōnion*). To ancient Greeks, a *daimōn* was usually good unless the context suggested otherwise, whereas a *daimōnion* was explicitly bad news. *Daimōnion* may also be a diminutive noun—like *duckling*, *piglet*, or *kitten*—and by using it with such overwhelming frequency, the gospel writers might be trying to convey the utter powerlessness of evil spirits when faced by Christ. Mocking demons and idols is a bit of a pastime in the Old Testament, like when Elijah trolls the prophets of Baal in 1 Kings 18:25–27 (read it, it's hilarious), or when the prophet Isaiah drops a twelve-verse idol taunt in Isaiah 44:9–20. Jesus is the man, and the biblical authors won't let you forget it.

That's the key point here. Demons are an active bunch in the Bible (particularly those who helped the Pharaoh's magicians in Exodus and the freaky medium of En-dor, who summons the spirit of "Samuel" in 1 Samuel 28) but they're absolutely nothing compared with Christ.

Just look at the things demon-possessed people say in the Bible:

"What have you to do with me, Jesus, Son of the Most High God?" (Mark 5:7; Luke 8:28)

"What have you to do with us, O Son of God?" (Matthew 8:29)

"You are the Son of God!" (Luke 4:41)

"I know who you are—the Holy One of God." (Mark 1:24 and Luke 4:34).

Demons, it seems, cannot help but proclaim the power of Jesus. In Acts 16:17, Paul is hounded for days by a fortune-telling slave girl with a spirit of divination that keeps telling the crowds, "These men are servants of the Most High God, who proclaim to you the way of salvation." Oh for more truth-tellers in our churches!

The uncomfortable reality is that demons often have a better theology than churchgoers. When the leader of the Jerusalem church is trying to help Jesus-followers understand that theoretical faith without good works is stillborn, he hammers home his point with this zinger: "You believe that there is one God. Good! Even the demons believe that—and shudder" (James 2:19 NIV). In other words, we are not saved by a head that assents to the idea that God is the boss. Even evil forces know this and hate it. Our heads *and* hearts must bow to Christ's lordship. We know it to be true in our mind, and we are delighted that it's true in our hearts.

We don't know how many demons there are in total, but the Bible mentions several *possible* individuals by name:

1. **Azazel**

In Leviticus 16:8–20, Aaron's two sons die due to blatant disobedience toward God. YHWH instructs Moses to have his brother make a sin offering for his house, saying, "Aaron shall cast lots over the two goats, one lot for the LORD and the other lot for Azazel. And Aaron shall present the goat on which the lot fell for the LORD and use it as a sin offering, but the goat on which the lot fell for Azazel shall be presented alive before the LORD to make atonement over it, that it may be sent away into the wilderness to Azazel" (vv. 8–10).

Post-biblical Jewish writing says Azazel taught humans how to make swords and oppress each other, and one apocalyptic passage even says Azazel was the Eden serpent. We don't know if Azazel is a demon, a place, a person, or a goat-shaped idol, or if the word *Azazel* just means scapegoat. One thing is for certain: God in His mercy offers Aaron a literal scapegoat for the nation's sin, and Azazel, if it is a demon, has zero power to atone for anything.

2. Belial

In 2 Corinthians 6:15, Paul asks the church at Corinth, "What accord has Christ with Belial? Or what portion does a believer share with an unbeliever?" It was Milton who popularized the notion that Belial is a fallen angel, but there's no other mention of Belial in the New Testament, and the Old Testament Hebrew word *beliyyaal* means worthlessness. Is Paul saying there's an actual demon named Worthless or is he just pointing out that there isn't any harmony between Jesus and any personification of worthlessness? Many Christians throughout history have conflated Accuser-Adversary and Belial as one and the same, but there isn't much solid ground for it.

3. Beelzebul

Baal-zebub, meaning "lord of the flies," is mentioned in one Old Testament passage (2 Kings 1:3–16), but this was probably just the Jewish way of making fun of a rival god of the Philistine city of Ekron, whose real name was Baal-zebul meaning "lord of princes." A "Beelzeboul" is also mentioned in the Testament of Solomon, a pseudepigraphical book containing a whole buffet of demons including one who sucks the thumbs of his victims. Solomon, so the story goes, possesses a ring that gives him the power to force demons to do his bidding.

In Matthew 12, Mark 3, and Luke 11, the Pharisees accuse Jesus of casting out demons by Beelzebul. Christ evidently gets the reference to the magical, demon-controlling ring. His response? "Behold, something greater than Solomon is here" (Matthew 12:42; Luke 11:31).

As with Belial, scores of Christians have insisted the Accuser-Adversary and Beelzebul are one and the same, but extra-biblical history makes that extremely unlikely.

4. Legion

We've already mentioned the Matthew 8:31 demons who go on to drown a herd of 2,000 pigs. The voice that speaks out of the cemetery-dwelling man called himself Legion, "for we are many" (Mark 5:9). Bear in mind that demons are liars. Do the demons not have individual names? Do they always travel together under one name? Or is Legion a single demon with multiple personalities? Or is this simply a not-so-subtle reference to the nearby Roman garrison? We don't know.

5. Mammon

Mammon is popularly (and likely inaccurately) known as the demon of greed and the god of money. In the Greco-Roman pantheon he is Plutus/Pluto, the god of wealth and the source word for the American and British political system of rule by the rich: *plutocracy*.

Mammon might be the most powerful and active of all the forces of darkness in our day, and it even seems to reside in many Western churches. Tens of millions of people who claim to be Christians grow richer with unjust gain thanks to ballooning pensions, portfolios, and retirement funds, the majority of which are teeming with shares in arms manufacturers, drug pushers, creation-killing energy monopolies, and banking bonds. Every day, churchgoers and non-churchgoers alike reap interest and profit off the backs of millions of members of the working poor, in direct violation of Scripture.

As 1 Timothy 6:10 puts it, "the love of money is a root of all kinds of evils." So long as people need money to survive, the powerful will leverage money to get others to sin for them, be it in engaging in cultural genocide for territorial expansion, human trafficking for prostitution, war for ideological imperium, environmental destruction for petrochemicals, or economic exploitation for shareholder profit.

It appears that Judas Iscariot was indwelled by Accuser-Adversary (Luke 22:3; John 13:27), partnering with darkness to betray his rabbi for hard cash (Matthew 26:14–16). How did Judas open up his heart to such evil? John 12:6 suggests it was his love of money.

One of the most stirring events in which Accuser-Adversary is mentioned is Acts 5:3. A churchgoing couple named Ananias and Sapphira decide to collude and con the Christian koinonia in Jerusalem by pretending to give wholeheartedly while secretly holding back some funds. The apostle Peter is appalled. "Ananias, why has Satan filled your heart to lie to the Holy Spirit and to keep back for yourself part of the proceeds of the land?" Both Ananias and Sapphira dropped dead on the spot.

But there's a tiny problem with the idea that Mammon is a demon or a god—it is not mentioned anywhere in the Bible.

Tertullian got the ball rolling on this idea by using the term *mammonas* to refer to an evil spirit. Gregory of Nyssa believed Mammon was another name for Beelzebul. John Chrysostom implied mammon was personified greed. There are whisperings of an ancient Syrian god named Mammon, but no evidence of this has ever surfaced. Mammon-as-demon-god-of-greed was popularized by Dante's *Divine Comedy* and seconded by Edmund Spenser's epic poem *The Faerie Queene*, and John Milton's *Paradise Lost* solidified the idea that Mammon was a fallen angel. Jacques Collin de Plancy's *Dictionnaire Infernal* suggests Mammon is hell's ambassador to Britain, which surely can't be far off the truth. Thomas Carlyle wrote a whole chapter on England's worship of money in his book *Past and Present*, entitled "Gospel of Mammonism." Mammon-as-demon makes a number of top ten lists throughout history, including the 1409 *Lanterne of Light*'s list of seven devils, the 1509 *De occulta philosophia*'s list of nine princes of devils, and the list of eight princes of hell in the 1589 *Treatise on Confessions by Evildoers and Witches*. But again, none of this is biblical.

Where did Christians get the idea that mammon is a demon or god? It comes down to Jesus's word choice. The two main words for money and wealth in the New Testament are *argurion* (twenty occurrences) and *chréma* (seven occurrences). Jesus uses *argurion* in places like Matthew 25:18 and Luke 19:15, and *chréma* in Mark 10:23 and Luke 18:24, but when making extremely important money points, He uses a word spoken *nowhere else* in Scripture besides Luke 16:9–13 and Matthew 6:24: *mammon*.

"No servant can serve two masters, for either he will hate the one and love the other, or he will be devoted to the one and despise the other. You cannot serve God and money [mammon]" (Luke 16:9–13; Matthew 6:24). Why does Jesus revert to His native tongue, Aramaic, for this one word? The fact that Jesus contrasts God with mammon led some Christians to think money must be a demon/god named Mammon. That might very well be the case, but the text never says so.

Do people act demonically and satanically with money? Absolutely, all the time. Money is often used in a satanic and demonic way, but the Bible never actually calls money a demon.

The etymology of the word *mammon* connotes strength in numbers. Mammon is the treasure in which we put our trust. Mammon equals wealth as trust. If you want to know if mammon still has a foothold in your life, ask the question, "If God asked me to give away 100 percent of my wealth and possessions right now, would I do it?" If the answer is anything less than an unflinching, joyous "Yes!" then there's still work to do. Ultimately, mammon is about self-trust instead of God-trust. What if money itself—our actual, manmade, and therefore fallen, projection of trust—wants to be our domineering master, wants us to love and serve and be devoted to it alone, and wants us to actively hate and despise God? Mammon might not be a demon, but it is demonic. As they say, the devil is in the details.

That's basically it for named demons in the Bible, plus perhaps Abaddon, Apollyon, Baal, and Moloch, but bear in mind that many of the named "demons" in Scriptures were also the gods of foreign nations, so there's no way to know who's who, exactly.

How many unnamed co-conspirators joined Accuser-Adversary in his coup plot? Thousands? Millions? Billions? We don't know for sure, but theologians tend to believe that a third of the angels joined Accuser-Adversary in his suicidal leap from grace. So how many total angels are there? Again, we don't know for sure. In Revelation 5:11, John reports seeing "myriads of myriads and thousands of thousands" of angels while other translations say "thousands upon thousands, and ten thousand times ten thousand." Daniel has a vision in Daniel 7:10 and reports the same, that "a thousand thousands served him, and ten thousand times ten thousand stood before him." If this is the case, then there are around a hundred million angels and perhaps thirty million fallen angels. In Matthew 26:53, when Peter is understandably freaking out as a mob sent by the high priestly house of Annas closes in on Jesus in the garden of Gethsemane, the rabbi tells His lead disciple that He can immediately summon 72,000 angels if He so desires. That's about as much as we have for an angelic-demonic census, but we really shouldn't put any stock in these likely symbolic numbers. The more important question: How do we get rid of them?

Demon Possession

Here's a toasty topic and a subject of hot debate: Can Christians be demon-possessed? I don't think so. Certainly not in the sense of ownership. Christians belong to Christ (Galatians 5:24)—they are literally and legally possessed by God. Demon possession is thought to occur when a demon takes total control of a human, such as in Luke 4:33–35 (where it makes a man scream in a synagogue that Jesus is the "Holy One of God"), Luke 8:27–33 (a naked man with super-human strength living in a cemetery), Acts

16:16–18 (a fortune-telling slave girl), and Matthew 17:14–18 (a demon causing a boy to experience what sounds like epileptic seizures). Can Accuser-Adversary have total and permanent control over a Christian's body, mind, and soul? I'm deeply skeptical. Remember 1 John 4:4—"Little children, you are from God and have overcome them [evil spirits], for he who is in you is greater than he who is in the world."

Nowhere in the Bible does it say Christians can be demon-possessed, and nowhere does Scripture teach how to cast demons out of a Christian. Christians can absolutely be influenced by the satanic and the demonic (Matthew 16:23), but there's not a single case of Christian demonic possession in the Word of God. How could Accuser-Adversary or any demon possess a life that is sealed by the Holy Spirit (2 Corinthians 1:22)? Why would God's Holy Spirit, a permanent resident in our bodies (1 Corinthians 6:19) want a roommate?

My theologian friend Richard John Saunders explains the nuance like this: A demon never owns a person, but a person may have a demon. A demon may exert influence or control over a person, but the responsibility is never taken from the person. As stated in the *Greek-English Lexicon of the New Testament Based on Semantic Domains*, "In a number of languages, one cannot speak of a person 'being possessed by a demon.' A more appropriate expression may be 'the person possesses a demon.' In other instances an idiomatic phrase is employed, 'the demon rides the person' or 'the demon commands the person.'"[2]

While ownership-possession is ruled out, that's not to say the demonic cannot *oppress* Christians at times. I asked my father about his encounter with "Mike" and the possibility of Christians being possessed, and his answer resonated. He said, "Christians who serve others through deliverance ministry say that when a believer in Jesus is experiencing demonic oppression, in extreme cases, it can functionally seem like possession: confused and clouded thoughts, inappropriate words, actions and behaviors all manifest the reality that something other than the person is controlling their faculties."

Remember, Accuser-Adversary only has two major tricks: He either gets us to seriously underestimate him or seriously overestimate him. If he can't afflict Christians with possession, he'll try for suppression or obsession. We give him far too much credit and neglect the roles that the world and the flesh play in our sinful choices. On one extreme, Christians will write off Accuser-Adversary and the demonic as purely symbolic; on the other extreme, Christians assume any slip or sin is an open invite for a full satanic indwelling. The Bible takes a far more balanced and far less dramatic approach. We simply put on the full armor of God (Ephesians 6:10–18), resist him (James 4:7), and he eventually goes away to regroup for another attack. Martin Luther agreed: "To be occupied with God's Word helps against the world, the flesh, and the Devil and all bad thoughts. This is the true holy water with which to exorcise the Devil."[3]

Exorcism

We see plenty of demon possessions in the Bible—eighty-one occurrences of the Greek *ekballo*, meaning to drive out, in the New Testament—but they're rarely like what we see in Hollywood movies. When was the last time an actor pretending to be demon-possessed said "Surely you are the Son of God?" This is the number one thing that *multiple* unclean spirits say to Jesus. Far from being dramatic, Jesus spends much of His interactions with demons telling them to zip their lips.

It's an uncomfortable truth for many Christians that Jesus is the most famous exorcist in the world, but there it is. Exorcisms are what made Jesus famous. Mark 1:32–39 records that Jesus healed so many people and cast out so many demons that the news spread until "Jesus could no longer openly enter a town" (Mark 1:45).

The presence of an unclean spirit or demon is usually much more subtle than a Hollywood flick: It manifests as insanity in Mark 5:1–5, sickness in Matthew 8:16–17, muteness in Matthew 9:32–34, blindness in Matthew 12:22, and epilepsy in Luke 9:37–43. Please note that physical ailments are not always caused by spirits—Jesus heals sickness without exorcism in Matthew 8:14–15 and blindness without exorcism in Matthew 9:27–81.

Also bear in mind that demon possession was exceedingly rare, even in Jesus's day. Jesus performs dozens of exorcisms in the Bible, but that's out of the tens of thousands of people He encounters over His years of public ministry. It's certainly less than 1 percent of the total number of people He feeds, heals, and teaches. Exorcist Gabriele Amorth, one of the founders of the International Association of Exorcists, is said to have carried out somewhere between 50,000 and 160,000 exorcisms, depending on the source you believe. (The priest and exorcist counted each prayer or ritual as an exorcism and assumed some people contained thousands of demons requiring hundreds of exorcisms.) To his credit, he always directed people to doctors and psychiatrists first, and believed that only ninety-four of his tens of thousands of encounters were genuine possessions, putting him roughly in line with Christ's ratio. In these cases, the signs are similar to those I've heard of in other cases in which the exorcist seems certain of demonic possession: enormous temporary strength, revealing knowledge about others in the room they don't know, and the ability to fluently speak foreign languages they don't understand.

The only exorcism performed by most Christians today is to essentially exorcise a belief in devils out of their churches and denominations. That said, demon-possession obsession still persists in lower-income churches. If your church's well-paved parking lot is packed with BMWs and Audis, you probably won't hear much about demons, but if you're in a Ford F-150s and Chevys, dirt road, Bibles-beers-and-bullets sort of church, there's a better chance in general that demon talk makes an appearance in the pulpit and balcony. That's not to say the rich churches are smarter and the poorer churches are less intelligent—I'm suggesting both are probably too extreme to be biblical.

Exorcism is a term widely used outside the church, but the preferred term on the Protestant end of things these days is *deliverance*. For Christians, deliverance is a last resort after all scientific options have been exhausted. Christian psychiatrists can even diagnose *possession syndrome*, a sort of dissociative disorder that leads patients to believe they're possessed, even if they actually aren't. God only knows for sure, so it's vital to approach all cases with humility and discernment.

Unlike what is shown in movies such as *The Exorcist*, exorcism is simply a form of prayer. There is nothing in the Bible that says you can only exorcise a demon with the help of Roman salt, garlic, or holy oil (though it does sound like the start of a very tasty pasta recipe). Silver crosses and incense aren't required for exorcism either, though they do remind one of the Old Testament's high priests making atonement for the nation's sins. Simply put, there is no drama in Jesus's prayers of exorcism. Frail ladies do not hurl fridges, little children do not climb walls, old men do not scream while bleeding from the eyes. No violence, no struggle, no magic. Christ remains calm and in absolute control. Why Christians make such a big deal of exorcism is beyond me. Many Christians pray a prayer of exorcism on a regular basis when they say the last line of the Lord's Prayer: "Deliver us from evil."

If anything, we need a little more exorcism in our churches these days. Don't we all need to be delivered from the world, the flesh, the demonic, and the satanic? Churches would do well to regularly exorcise the collective demonic and satanic—that which is accusatory or adversarial to God's way. The love of money would be an excellent place to start. After all, what is the climax of Jesus's ministry that serves as the catalyst for His arrest and execution? Driving out the economic exploiters from the temple (Mark 11:15–18; Matthew 21:12–13; Luke 19:45–46; John 2:13–16). All four accounts use the term for exorcism (*ekballo*) here, to drive out. Jesus drove the love of money out of the house of God and the religious elite hated Him for it.

Christians need to be delivered from all sorts of possessions—anxiety (Philippians 4:6), the past (Philippians 3:13–14), the love of the world (1 John 2:15–16), unforgiveness (Ephesians 4:32), our own understanding (Proverbs 3:5), false teaching (Galatians 1:8), and human approval (Galatians 1:10). We need to take the spiritual dimension seriously, and we need to make zero-drama exorcism popular again.

We also need to be exorcised of the spirit of demonization.

Demonization

> We, with Allah's help, call on every Muslim who believes in Allah and wishes to be rewarded to comply with Allah's order to kill the Americans and plunder their money wherever and whenever they find it. We also call on Muslim ulema, leaders, youths, and soldiers to launch the raid on Satan's U.S. troops and the devil's supporters allying with them.
>
> —Osama bin Laden, World Islamic Front Statement,
> February 23, 1998

On January 13, 2010, just two days after an earthquake killed 200,000 people in Haiti, fundamentalist televangelist Pat Robertson went on *The 700 Club* and informed America that "Something happened a long time ago in Haiti, and people might not want to talk about it. They were under the heel of the French. Uh, you know, Napoleon III or whatever. And they got together and swore a pact to the devil. They said, 'We will serve you if you will get us free from the French.' True story. And so, the devil said, 'OK, it's a deal.' And uh, they kicked the French out. You know, the Haitians revolted and got themselves free. But ever since, they have been cursed by one thing after the other."[4]

In 2010, Dove World Outreach Center in Florida received global press coverage when it announced their "International Burn a Koran Day." On March 20, 2011, they followed through and burned a Qur'an. A few days later, Muslims in Afghanistan attacked a UN Assistance Mission and murdered twelve people. Both sides declared the other to be demonic, and perhaps both were right.

An ancient witch-hunter's bible called *Malleus Malificarum* suggested women are more genetically predisposed to do the devil's bidding than men. During the Inquisition, a third nipple was a sure sign of satanic involvement.

When William Blake wrote *The Marriage of Heaven and Hell*, he demonized John Milton by saying, "The reason Milton wrote in fetters when he wrote of Angels & God, and at liberty when of Devils & Hell, is because he was a true Poet and of the Devils party without knowing it."[5]

Martin Luther called the pope the Antichrist in his 1520 work *Against the Execrable Bull of the Antichrist*. Perhaps he was right, or perhaps one or both were acting like antichrists.

It's easy to demonize people with whom we disagree. We've seen images of both Bush and Obama with horns. The Islamic world regularly calls America "the great Satan." When former Venezuelan president Hugo Chavez spoke at the United Nations the day after George W. Bush, he remarked, "Yesterday the devil was here . . . it still smells of sulfur."[6] The audience was shocked at first, but then broke into laughter and applause until they were told to stop.

If there is one person on earth who is actually fit to claim someone else is demon possessed, it's the holy, righteous, all-knowing Jesus of Nazareth. And yet Jesus doesn't claim it is the Romans, Samaritans, Gentiles, or Greeks who are in cahoots with Accuser-Adversary, but the so-called faithful Jewish religious elite. When Jesus hurls accusations of devil-dealings, it's usually in connection with the Jewish religious elite—the conservative Pharisees, the liberal Sadducees, the conniving lawyer-scribes, the aristocratic elders, and above all, the wicked high priestly crime family led by the murderous Annas ben Sethi that I discuss in *A God Named Josh*. Consider John 8. Jesus is teaching in the Jerusalem temple courts near the treasury. He's surrounded by religious Jews. Verse 30 says many believed in Him, but in verse 44 He says, "You are of your father the devil, and your will is to do your father's desires. He was a murderer from the beginning, and does not stand in the truth, because there is no truth in him. When he lies, he speaks out of his own character, for he is a liar and the father of lies." Four verses later, they accuse Jesus of being demon possessed. By verse 52 they are sure of it. By verse 59, they pick up stones to throw at Him and Jesus hides and leaves the area.

The reality is that any non-Christian can fall into demonic and devilish habits, as 1 John 3:8 makes clear: "Whoever makes a practice of sinning is of the devil, for the devil has been sinning from the beginning. The reason the Son of God appeared was to destroy the works of the devil."

Ironically, it is often those who promise to purge evil—even genuinely real evil—that end up perpetrating the most evil. Think Mao Zedong's mass eradication of landlords during the Land Reform Movement, Oliver Cromwell's killing of royalists during the Commonwealth, Joseph Stalin's execution of communists during the Great Purge, and according to Brown University's Costs of War Project, the killing of 432,000 civilians and the displacement of 38 million more in the US quest to purge the Taliban and al-Qaeda after 9/11 (and secure their oil exports, of course).[7] It's the religious elite who accuse Jesus of being demon-possessed, and it's the demonizers who end up partnering with Accuser-Adversary-filled Judas to murder the Son of God.

Demonizing others—ascribing absolute good to team Us and absolute evil to team Them—is grounds for disaster. Demonization battering rams open the door to dehumanization. They are evil. We are good. Doesn't God want the destruction of evil? Then we'd best get to work destroying people created in the image of God. It's a story we've seen time and again in Islam, Catholicism, and a hundred other worldviews. How can creatures so *not* all-knowing possibly have the final answer on someone else's goodness or badness? How can we demonize someone created in the image of God? When we give in to that temptation—to target the human instead of realizing we aren't fighting against flesh and blood—we open ourselves up to becoming the very thing we're accusing others of being. This might be why Jesus says only God is good (Mark 10:18; Luke 18:19) and that we should let Him sort the wheat from the weeds at the end of days (Matthew 13:30). The brutal reality is that we have all sinned and fallen short of the glory of God (Romans 3:23). There is only One being who has the right and ability to search the human heart, and we shouldn't assume that person is us.

Lord, please deliver us from the demon of demonization.

PART III

WORK AND LOCATION

6

HEAVEN'S HIERARCHY

"It is all a mysterious realm, thrown into confusion by an unhappy
drama about which we know very little."

—Pope Paul VI, *Deliver Us from Evil*

BEFORE WE CAN TALK about the devil, we need to talk about God.
The spiritual world has an org chart, so to speak, and it's important we don't place Accuser-Adversary too high or too low in the
pecking order. Heaven's hierarchy:

God the Father, God the Son, God the Holy Spirit
The divine council
The angel of the Lord
Archangels
Angels – Cherubim – Seraphim – Lucifers – Satans
Principalities and powers
Accuser-Adversary – fallen angels/demons – antichrists – beasts

The Trinity

Everything, including Accuser-Adversary, finds its source in God
and exists for His ultimate plans and purposes. The Christian God

is One, but because He's so intensely relational, He's a three-in-one. God the Father is known to us as YHWH, often pronounced Yahweh or Jehovah. God the Son is Jesus Christ; His earthly Hebrew name was Yehoshua ben Yehoseph, and He is known as Jesus of Nazareth. God the Holy Spirit is sent by God the Father through God the Son to dwell in Christians as we speak. God the Father, God the Son, and God the Holy Spirit are co-equals and co-eternal persons. The Father is not the Son, the Son is not the Holy Spirit, and the Holy Spirit is not the Father, but the Father is God, the Son is God, and the Holy Spirit is God. Perhaps the closest human analogy we can conjure is that of water. Water the river is not water the lake is not water the ocean, but the ocean is water, the lake is water, and the river is water. It still falls wildly short, but it's a glimpse at least.

The Trinity is never explicitly mentioned in the Bible, but He can be triangulated across the library of Scripture. (Homework: Check out Genesis 1:1–2; Genesis 1:26; Isaiah 9:6; Zechariah 12:10; Isaiah 48:16; Matthew 28:19; John 10:30; 2 Corinthians 13:14; Colossians 2:9; 1 Peter 1:2; John 14:16–17; Ephesians 4:4–6; Hebrews 9:14.)

Humans could never possibly wrap their minds around a being so infinite that He essentially calls himself *Being Itself* in Exodus 3:14. We have a hard time envisioning a solar system or the atoms in our sandwich, let alone the Creator of existence and the universe. God is simply beyond all human comprehension.

One of the key attributes of the triune God is His relationality. The trinity "works all things according to the counsel of his will" (Ephesians 1:11) which, for whatever reasons He saw fit, includes a divine council of created beings.

The Divine Council

In Genesis 1:26, God says, "Let us make man in our image, after our likeness. And let them have dominion over the fish of the sea and over the birds of the heavens and over the livestock and over all the earth and over every creeping thing that creeps on the earth." Who is God talking to? Some scholars think He was talking to members of His divine council. (My strong sense is that God is talking to himself—He's a trinity, after all.)

As an accommodation for humans who cannot possibly fathom the heavenlies, God's council is patterned in terms of an ancient king's courtly throne room. Multiple Old Testament writers have visions of this mysterious divine council. It's a patchwork mosaic, but let's try to paint the picture in our minds (fair warning: the scene is, frankly, terrifying).

First, the heavenly courtroom itself, as described in Ezekiel 1:4–6, 22, 26–28.

> As I looked, behold, a stormy wind came out of the north, and a great cloud, with brightness around it, and fire flashing forth continually, and in the midst of the fire, as it were gleaming metal. And from the midst of it came the likeness of four living creatures. And this was their appearance: they had a human likeness, but each had four faces, and each of them had four wings. . . .
>
> Over the heads of the living creatures there was the likeness of an expanse, shining like awe-inspiring crystal, spread out above their heads. . . .
>
> And above the expanse over their heads there was the likeness of a throne, in appearance like sapphire; and seated above the likeness of a throne was a likeness with a human appearance. And upward from what had the appearance of his waist I saw as it were gleaming metal, like the appearance of fire enclosed all around. And downward from what had the appearance of his waist I saw as it were the appearance of fire, and there was brightness around him. Like the appearance of the bow that is in the cloud on the day of rain, so was the appearance of the brightness all around.
>
> Such was the appearance of the likeness of the glory of the LORD. And when I saw it, I fell on my face.

Revelation 4:2–6 offers a nearly identical image, except with the addition of an emerald rainbow, twenty-four elders seated on thrones, lightning and thunder from God's throne, and a sea of glass before it.

What does God look like in this scene? Daniel 7:9–10 reports,

> As I looked, thrones were placed,
> and the Ancient of Days took his seat;
> his clothing was white as snow,
> and the hair of his head like pure wool;
> his throne was fiery flames;
> its wheels were burning fire.
> A stream of fire issued and came out from before him;
> a thousand thousands served him, and ten thousand
> times ten thousand stood before him;
> the court sat in judgment,
> and the books were opened.

Additional passages in Ezekiel 1 and 10 mention God's fiery throne is on wheels, and that spirits dart to and fro and follow His spirit wherever He goes. In other words, God's throne room is a moveable kingdom.

In Psalm 82:1, Asaph says, "God has taken his place in the divine council; in the midst of the gods he holds judgment." It appears these other gods are less than perfect, because Asaph declares in verses 6 and 7, "I said, 'You are gods, sons of the Most High, all of you; nevertheless, like men you shall die, and fall like any prince.'"

How often does God gather this council? How often does He hold court? Fairly regularly, based on the scriptural evidence. Job 1:6 and Job 2:1 lists two separate times when "the sons of God came to present themselves before the LORD," and Accuser-Adversary is specifically named in both instances.

In Jeremiah 23:18 and 22, YHWH inveighs against lying prophets: "For who among them has stood in the council of the

LORD to see and to hear his word, or who has paid attention to his word and listened? . . . if they had stood in my council, then they would have proclaimed my words to my people, and they would have turned them from their evil way, and from the evil of their deeds."

In Isaiah 6, God has a message for Israel and from His throne asks in verse 8, "Whom shall I send, and who will go for us?"

In 1 Kings 22:19–23, Micaiah has a vision of this council, too:

> I saw the LORD sitting on his throne, and all the host of heaven standing beside him on his right hand and on his left; and the LORD said, "Who will entice Ahab, that he may go up and fall at Ramoth-gilead?" And one said one thing, and another said another. Then a spirit came forward and stood before the LORD, saying, "I will entice him." And the LORD said to him, "By what means?" And he said, "I will go out, and will be a lying spirit in the mouth of all his prophets." And he said, "You are to entice him, and you shall succeed; go out and do so." Now therefore behold, the LORD has put a lying spirit in the mouth of all these your prophets; the LORD has declared disaster for you.

As these books suggest, God has a divine council—an awesome, massive, terrifying court. This is not a democratic congress, a republic, a monarchy, or even an emperor's throne room. Notice the overlapping elements in many of these visions. Pair those with Revelation 5 and 6 and you get a glimpse behind the curtain at ultimate reality. No matter how bad things are looking on earth—be it famine, persecution, war, or a church in freefall—God is on His throne, the slain Lamb lives and rules and is worthy to open the scrolls. This is more than just a potential vision of the future—this is an alternate view of the here and now. This is a heavenly council containing angels and demons and rainbows and fire and throngs of spirits and the thunderous presence of God himself. It seems almost unnecessary for the writer of Psalm 96:9 to say we should "Worship the LORD in the splendor of holiness; tremble before him, all the earth!" How could we possibly do anything else?

Angels

Before we can talk about devils and demons, we need to talk about angels. The Hebrew word for angel is *malak* (pronounced mal-awk), which appears 213 times in the Old Testament, and it means messenger. In a huge number of cases, the *malak* is human, so it is translated as "messenger." Moses sends messengers (*malakim*, angels) to the king of Edom in Numbers 20:14. Only Rahab the prostituted woman was spared from the fall of Jericho in Joshua 6:17 because she hid the messengers—Joshua's two spies. Gideon sent messengers to recruit soldiers in Judges 6:35. In 1 Samuel 6:21, the sickly citizens of Beth-shemesh sent messengers to the people of Kiriath-jearim to take the ark of the covenant off their hands. In 2 Samuel 11:23, a "messenger" reported to King David that the assassination of Bathsheba's Uriah had been completed. In 1 Kings 19:2, the wicked queen Jezebel sent a "messenger" to Elijah, promising to kill him "by this time tomorrow." In Psalm 104:4, the psalmist (probably David) envisions even the wind can be a "messenger" of YHWH. As if to make abundantly clear that humans can be "messengers" (*malakim*, angels), Haggai 1:13 specifically names Haggai the prophet as a malak of God. Malachi then prophesies in Malachi 3:1 that God will send another "messenger" to prepare the way for His arrival.

The trick for Bible translators, of course, is trying to discern which of these *malakim* are human messengers and which are heavenly messengers. In Genesis 19:1, two "angels" warn Lot to get out of Sodom before it gets roasted to cinder. In Exodus 33:2, YHWH promises Moses He'll send an "angel" ahead of Israel to help drive out the wicked nations. (Exodus 23:28 suggests God uses hornets.) In Psalm 78:49, the psalmist Asaph suggests God has at least one band of destroying "angels," while the psalmist of Psalm 91:11 (possibly Moses) assumes there are also guardian "angels."

How many angels are there? We don't know. David envisions heaven's army consisting of at least 20,000 chariots (Psalm 68:17). There may be thousands (Hebrews 12:22), tens of thousands (Psalm 68:17), or even tens of millions (Revelation 5:11). More than likely, these numbers are estimates or purely symbolic.

The Angel of the Lord

The most active of the angels is definitely God's personal representative. This special angel is mentioned around one hundred times in the Old Testament and is referred to as either "the angel of God" or "the angel of the LORD." In other words, this is YHWH's personal ambassador. This does not necessarily mean a winged being flying down from heaven. The angel of YHWH appears to Moses in a blazing fire within a bush in Exodus 3:2 (and two verses later, it's God himself). The angel of YHWH appears to Hagar (in a dream? in human likeness?) by a desert spring in Genesis 16:7 and promised to multiply her offspring (which actually happened, as her son Ishmael became an ancestor of the Arab nations). A female donkey spots the angel of YHWH blocking the road with a sword in Numbers 22:23. This one gets crazier—the text in Numbers 22:22 says the *malak* of YHWH took his stand against Balaam *as a satan*. When Gideon cooks a meal for the angel of YHWH in Judges 6:21, the angel's staff sparks fire from the rock and then he disappears. As we can imagine, sometimes people were confused by what they saw. In Judges 13:3, the angel of YHWH appears to Samson's mom, and three verses later she tells her husband that she met a man who *looked* like the angel of God. When the fellow reappears to both of them in Judges 13:19, Manoah burns an offering and the angel of YHWH ascends on the flame in verse 20. Clearly, this angelic representation of God is powerful, because many of the humans who encounter it freak out as though they've seen God himself.

We don't know how many heavenly angels there are in total, but the Bible mentions several possible individuals by name:

1. *Michael*

Michael is mentioned five times in the Bible. He's the only angel listed as the archangel (Jude 1:9), suggesting he's heaven's top dog as far as angels are concerned. He has an army of angels at his disposal (Revelation 12:7) and he is strong enough to take on national demons (Daniel 10:13). Anyone whose name is written in the book (i.e., Christians) is under his princely protection (Daniel 12:1) and he contends for Israel alongside God (Daniel 10:21). Michael has a healthy respect for Accuser-Adversary, even when fighting him for Moses's body (Jude 1:9), but that will not stop him and his angels from trouncing Accuser-Adversary when war breaks out in heaven (Revelation 12:7–9). When the Lord returns, it will be with the voice of an archangel (1 Thessalonians 4:16).

2. *Gabriel*

Gabriel is mentioned four times in the Bible, and is sometimes nicknamed the Christmas Angel because he's the fellow who gets to announce Christ's incarnation to Mary (Luke 1:26–33). He also announces the pregnancy of Elizabeth with John the Baptizer to the father Zechariah (Luke 1:11–17). Gabriel has access to the presence of God (Luke 1:19) and the power to make men mute for months (Luke 1:20). He might be the same angel who announces the news of Christ's birth to the shepherds in Luke 2:9–10, but the text doesn't say. He can take on the appearance of a man (Daniel 8:15–16) and has the ability to help humans understand visions (Daniel 8:16–26). He can fly (Daniel 9:21), prophesy about the future (Daniel 9:20–27), and every earthling who encounters him is rightly terrified.

That's it for named angels, unless you include Accuser-Adversary. Commonly named angels from extra-biblical literature include Raphael and Uriel, along with Raguel, Sariel, and Remiel. The apocryphal book of Jubilees in 15:25–27 reports the oddly specific detail that angels were created already circumcised.

Next up are the angels of nature, churches, and nations. Even Jesus has an angel (Revelation 1:1) and says so explicitly in Revelation 22:16—"I, Jesus, have sent my angel to testify to you about these things for the churches."

The angels of nature

Revelation 7:1 lists four angels with the ability to control the wind. Revelation 16:5 says there's an angel in charge of the waters. Revelation 19:17 describes an angel standing in the sun. Are these angels all metaphors and symbols or are they real spiritual beings? We don't know.

The angels of churches

The Bible lists seven real churches, all in modern-day Turkey, who had angels: Ephesus, Smyrna, Pergamum, Thyatira, Sardis, Philadelphia, and Laodicea (Revelation 2:1–3:16). Some people have speculated that the angel in Acts 8:26 represented the church in Jerusalem and the angel in Acts 10:3 represented Caesarea, but the text doesn't expressly say so.

It's fascinating to think that maybe all churches have angels, that these spiritual realities might represent the collective spirituality of the congregation. What might your church's angel be like? Has the angel of my church been around for eons or did it come to life when the church was planted 144 years ago? If our church does have an enduring collective spirit, it prefers a pastor-centric model and can't yet let go of member voting and entrust the church's leadership to its elders. And don't dare bring up the removal of pews! That said, it is also a deeply gentle, kind, and loving angel committed to caring for the young, the old, the weak, and the sick. It is an angel who loves heartiness and friends and longs for revival in the nation.

The angels of nations

Nations, too, can have angels.

Deuteronomy 32:8 says, "When the Most High gave to the nations their inheritance, when he divided mankind, he fixed the borders of the peoples according to the number of the sons of God."

An angel tells Daniel, "The prince of the kingdom of Persia withstood me twenty-one days, but Michael, one of the chief princes, came to help me, for I was left there with the kings of Persia" (Daniel 10:13). A few verses later, the angel alludes to a coming battle with the prince in charge of Greece (Daniel 10:20). God claims Israel as His personal protectorate in Deuteronomy 32:9. Daniel 10:21 says Michael is the angel of God's holy nation, the household of faith. Isaiah 14 suggests there was a dark angel animating the king of Babylon, and Ezekiel 28 suggests something similar about the king of Tyre. Isaiah 19 might be referring to Egypt's angel. Revelation 9:14 says there are four angels "bound at the great river Euphrates," which might refer to Turkey, Syria, Iraq, and Iran. (In the following verses, these four angels amass an army of 200 million soldiers and slaughter a third of humanity.)

What might your national angel be like? Does the United Kingdom have an ancient aristocorporatist feudalist ruler who refuses to let Britons shake free from serfdom? Does Canada's relatively new angel keep hyper-individualist minds fixed on rampant consumerism and its attendant world-topping per capita consumer debt levels? Does America's angel pride itself on being the exception to every rule?

Is Accuser-Adversary himself the angel of any nation? Revelation 12 and 13 seem to suggest he was the god of Rome at the time of writing. Perhaps Accuser-Adversary becomes the angel of the global superpower de jour. Maybe America really is the so-called great satan, for now at least, and perhaps Accuser-Adversary is starting to stalk his way east toward China. Or perhaps Accuser-Adversary takes a multinational approach. Ephesians 2:2 appears to refer to him as "the prince of the power of the air." John 12:31 calls him "the ruler of this world," and 2 Corinthians 4:4 calls him "the god of this world."

Demons

We covered demons, demon possession, demonization, and exorcisms in chapter 5, but demons are angels who chose self-will and rebellion instead of fidelity to God—see Jude 1:6; 2 Peter 2:4; and Revelation 12:7–9—though all three of those passages continue to call them angels and not demons.

Antichrist

Among the fallen angels, Accuser-Adversary looms largest, but there's another named demon of sorts: the Antichrist. The word is *antichristos* in Greek, and it means "the one who opposes the messiah." Haven't we all been an antichrist at some point?

First John 2:18 says, "Children, it is the last hour, and as you have heard that antichrist is coming, so now many antichrists have come." Anyone who denies Jesus is the Christ is the antichrist (1 John 2:22). Every spirit that refuses to confess Jesus is from God is the spirit of the antichrist (1 John 4:3). Those who don't believe God came down as Jesus is the antichrist (2 John 1:7). So who is the capital-A Antichrist? Is it an individual person or a collective representation? Perhaps a helpful way to look at it: Christians are a collective entity called the church, indwelled with the spirit of Christ. Non-Christians are a collective entity called antichrist, indwelled with the spirit of sin. Perhaps. The Bible is clear that there are many antichrists. Before I became a Christian, I was an antichrist. So were you. Anyone who denies Jesus Christ is an antichrist. We'll discuss the specific Antichrist being in chapter 11, "The End: Part One."

Nephilim

Another type of being sometimes considered to be a possible form of fallen angel are the Nephilim mentioned in Genesis 6:1–4.

> When man began to multiply on the face of the land and daughters were born to them, the sons of God saw that the daughters of man were attractive. And they took as their wives any they chose. Then the LORD said, "My Spirit shall not abide in man forever, for he is flesh: his days shall be 120 years." The Nephilim were on the earth in those days, and also afterward, when the sons of God came in to the daughters of man and they bore children to them. These were the mighty men who were of old, the men of renown.

The word Nephilim also derives from the Hebrew word *naphal*, meaning "fallen." Also note the tidy literary contrast between the sons of God and the daughters of man. Their argument is that the phrase "sons of God" is a reference to angelic beings in Job 1:6, 2:1, and 38:7, even though it's a different word. Some scholars think the whole point of Noah's flood was to wash away these so-called half-human half-demon demigods. I'd simply add that the sons of God and the Nephilim are not to be conflated, and we probably shouldn't overcomplicate things. Genesis 6:1–4 seems to simply suggest that godly people started marrying unbelievers during the time of the giants.

It's all speculation. In Hosea 1:10, God calls Israelites "Children of the living God." Hebrews 1:5 asks, "For to which of the angels did God ever say, 'You are my Son, today I have begotten you'? Or again, 'I will be to him a father, and he shall be to me a son'?" In Matthew 5:9, Jesus says peacemakers will be called the sons of God. Romans 8:14 says all those who are led by the Holy Spirit are sons of God. Plus, Jesus says in Matthew 22:30 that angels don't do marriage. Justin Martyr believed the angels first sinned through their sexual desire for women, though how exactly a spiritual being derives physical pleasure has caused theological head-scratching for centuries. According to Justin Martyr in his *Second Apology*, the offspring of those angel daddies are the demons who pollute humanity to this day.

Does the Bible support this idea? Both 2 Peter 2:4–6 and Jude 6–7 seem to suggest fallen angels indulged in some sort of sexual perversion. Perhaps the phrase "sons of God" really does mean fallen angels and there was a mixed race prior to the flood, but the text is fairly clear that those sons of God were not Nephilim. The word *Nephilim* means "giants," specifically, the tall and presumably muscular sons of Anak mentioned in Numbers 13:33. The Israelite warrior Joshua destroys most of the Anakim in Joshua 11:21–22, and Goliath comes from one of the three Anakim cities that survived (1 Samuel 17:4). If there were half-man-half-demons and Noah's flood was supposed to wipe them out, it evidently didn't work (Numbers 13:33).

Humans

Make no mistake—we Homo sapiens are spiritual beings just as much as we are physical beings.

Humans must have seemed incredibly strange to Accuser-Adversary when we first came on the scene. Unlike angelic beings—who sometimes have six wings (Isaiah 6:2–7), sometimes are covered in eyes (Ezekiel 10:12), and sometimes are embedded with expensive jewels (Ezekiel 28:13)—these new fleshy beings bore the unmistakable image of the God against whom Accuser-Adversary had rebelled. Humans were a constant reminder of the One he's trying to replace. All the more reason to hate the earthlings. Worse still, these new beings could create more image-bearing beings simply by joining their bodies together in pleasure. Yuck. Accuser-Adversary would need to find ways to pervert this pleasure to minimize the number of God-looking beings he'd have to face for the rest of his earth-dwelling days.

God adds insult to injury by giving these new image-bearers dominion over the physical earth in Genesis 1:26. "Then God said, 'Let us make man in our image, after our likeness. And let them have dominion over the fish of the sea and over the birds of the heavens and over the livestock and over all the earth and over every creeping thing that creeps on the earth.'"

Who was God talking to? He very much seems to be talking to His Trinity self again. Let *us* make man in *our* image. Let's give them dominion. Near-total control, mastery, stewardship. Let's make them the caretakers of all creation. Their job is not to assume the status quo is good, but to conform all things to the word, will, and way of their God. Will they remain faithful? Or will they be led astray and rebel?

From the very start, humans chose rebellion.

So that's the playground in which Accuser-Adversary is tasked to work. As we'll see in the next chapter, he has plenty of powers and plenty of limits on his powers, and quite frustratingly for him, even his every act of rebellion still works to serve God.

7

THE DEVIL INCARNATE

"We may not pay Satan reverence, for that would be indiscreet,
but we can at least respect his talents."

—Mark Twain, *Concerning the Jews*

SEPTIMIA ZENOBIA WAS A WOMAN with ambition. The third-century Syrian queen wasn't satisfied to rule the city state of Palmyra mentioned in 2 Chronicles 8:4. She wanted an empire of her own. There was only one problem: She was born in the age of the Roman Empire. Her kingdom was a client kingdom of Rome, and she chafed under a higher authority. So she rebelled. In 269 AD, she invaded and conquered the Roman province of Egypt. The following year, she invaded and conquered vast lands that now form Syria, Iraq, Turkey, Egypt, Jordan, Lebanon, Israel, Palestine, and Saudi Arabia. Her goal was an empire to rival Rome, and for a time she achieved it. Zenobia grew the expanse of her empire eighteen-fold and soon ruled 734,000 square miles from modern-day Iraq to Egypt. After the Romans unsuccessfully tried to retake Egypt and Syria in 271 AD, she declared herself "Augusta" (empress) of the new Palmyrene Empire and stamped her brag on coins for good measure.

Roman retribution came swiftly and brutally. In 272 AD, Aurelian's armies broke Zenobia's army, captured the queen, and leveled Palmyra. Ironically, though Zenobia had spent her short-lived rule in rebellion against Rome, in the end it led to an *expansion* of the Roman Empire, not only after it captured her ally Armenia, but because she'd brought authority and stability to the region that inadvertently secured Rome's eastern frontier. In the end, Zenobia earned Aurelian the title of Restorer of the East.

Accuser-Adversary may have quit heaven, but he still has a job to do in service to the King of Kings and Lord of Lords. Based on the English name we've given him, sharp readers will already know exactly what Accuser-Adversary does for a living: He tests and accuses Christians. As we've seen, Accuser-Adversary only definitively appears five times in the entire Bible, and in three of these appearances, he's working in the role of tester. He tests and accuses Job, he tests and accuses Joshua, he tests and accuses Jesus. You could also argue that he tests Judas, but unlike the other three Js, Judas fails terribly.

Aside from Job, Joshua, Jesus, and Judas, plus possibly David in 1 Chronicles 21 and Eve in Genesis, I'd argue that Accuser-Adversary also tested Simon Peter and the disciples in Luke 22:31. Jesus says to Peter, "Simon, Simon, behold, Satan demanded to have you [plural], that he might sift you [plural] like wheat."

It's worth noting that Accuser-Adversary isn't the only tester of Christians. God himself tests (*but doesn't tempt*) people:

Jeremiah 17:10: "I the LORD search the heart and test the mind, to give every man according to his ways, according to the fruit of his deeds."

Jeremiah 9:6–7: "Heaping oppression upon oppression, and deceit upon deceit, they refuse to know me, declares the LORD. Therefore thus says the LORD of hosts: 'Behold,

I will refine them and test them, for what else can I do, because of my people?'"

1 Chronicles 29:17: "I know, my God, that you test the heart and have pleasure in uprightness. In the uprightness of my heart I have freely offered all these things, and now I have seen your people, who are present here, offering freely and joyously to you."

Psalm 26:2: "Prove me, O LORD, and try me; test my heart and my mind."

Psalm 139:23: "Search me, O God, and know my heart! Try me and know my thoughts!"

God tests. Accuser-Adversary tempts. Sometimes at the same time. God tests for our good, but the devil tempts for our undoing.

Thanks to our horrible modern industrial-corporate education complex, most of us grew up with a serious phobia of tests, if not a downright hatred of them. Even as adults, we loathe math tests, university qualification tests, driving tests, career tests, and health tests.

But is good testing really all that bad? Consider John Wooden, the famous UCLA basketball coach who won more NCAA championships than any other coach, including seven straight wins. Not everyone who could bounce a basketball got to play for the Wizard of Westwood. Tryouts were tests to see if you were good enough to make the team. Practices were tests to see if you were good enough to stay on the team. Games were tests to see if you were good enough to be a starter. Over thousands of practices and games, Wooden tested his players and trained them into an elite game-winning machine.

Righteous testing can even save your life. The US Navy doesn't let just any amateur swimmer become a Navy Seal. They put candidates through a series of tests. The first test is a basic physical screening test (PST), in which candidates have forty-eight minutes to swim 500 yards, do fifty pushups, fifty sit-ups, ten pull-ups, and a 1.5-mile run. Only 25 percent of those who pass the PST will survive the gauntlet that is Hell Week, a brutal 5.5-day trial during which entrants do more than twenty hours of physical training per day, run more than 200 miles carrying backpacks, boats, and logs, spend hours in the cold sea, and do it all on less than four hours of sleep for the entire week. During this testing ordeal, commanding officers tempt them to quit, and the vast majority do. Is there far too much sadomasochistic motive in militaries? Yes, of course. But there is also a purely practical motive: The Navy tests to ensure fitness and fortitude so that, come live warfare in an open battle, these same men and women won't die. Testing and tempting during training can and does save lives.

Pure-motives testing is a wonderful way to safely prepare for the challenges of life. The CIA and MI6 test their spies to make sure they remain faithful to their respective homelands and don't become double agents. Chiefs of staff do debate prep with their presidential candidates, brutally assailing them so when they get on stage they can remain collected and make their points without getting rattled. From 1587 to 1983, the Catholic Church employed a devil's advocate to test the worthiness of anyone proposed for sainthood, so as to ensure only the loftiest of fallen humans could ascend to canonization. Even temptation can have a righteous motive: A parent can leave out a chocolate bar or some coins to test the obedience or integrity of their children. Their goal isn't to exasperate or provoke their kids (Colossians 3:21) but to cultivate their character and virtue.

But unlike a godly parent, smart coach, chief spy, or military unit, Accuser-Adversary does not have right motives. He may have started as a righteous tester, but he has turned into a terrible tempter. And that's just the start.

Tester Turns Accuser

Accuser-Adversary was supposed to test us, and then bring truthful allegations before the Lord if human inconsistencies arose. Instead, he tempts us and then accuses us regardless of the outcome. Like a naughty child, he practices the trap-and-tattletale. Please do not make the mistake of thinking Accuser-Adversary spends all of his time tormenting and terrorizing unbelieving individuals here on Earth. Revelation 12:10 says the devil spends much of his time in heaven doing his job: accusing Christians "day and night before our God." Accuser-Adversary doesn't need to accuse nonbelievers because they're already on his side. There's no point in saying "Hey, God, Kim Jong Un is still running a slave plantation called North Korea." Instead, Accuser-Adversary stomps back and forth to the courtroom of heaven, hurling accusations at Christians in hopes of securing permission to test the trueness of their faith. But even as he points out our incalculable imperfections, pathetic weaknesses, hidden sins, and outright hypocrisies, we mercifully have a public defender to advocate before God on our behalf. It is none other than the risen Savior himself: "My little children, I am writing these things to you so that you may not sin. But if anyone does sin, we have an advocate with the Father, Jesus Christ the righteous" (1 John 2:1).

Jesus Christ the righteous. When Accuser-Adversary screams "Unrighteous," Jesus our advocate counters, "Nonsense. This human is a child of the King. She is perfectly righteous due to her faith in me." God bangs His gavel. Case dismissed. The devil continues to fume and is found in contempt of court for the ump-teenth time. God lays a verbal smackdown like in Zechariah 3:2, and right before Michael the bailiff heads in his direction, Accuser-Adversary slinks off to find another Christian to accuse. Notice there is no devil's advocate. Jesus is our advocate and He always gets the final word.

Do you feel how real this heavenly courtroom is? Deep down, I think everybody does. Tim Keller, in his beautiful sermon *Accuser and the Advocate*, says, "There is a courtroom. And there is an accuser. And there is a bar of justice. And we are actually being accused there. And we know it. And our conscience is a radio transmitter picking up the prosecution."[1]

Sadly, Accuser-Adversary's work of accusation has become the church's favorite pastime. I will be the first to admit that I play the Accuser-Adversary's role—that of accusing Christians of unfaithfulness instead of considering others more significant than myself (Philippians 2:3)—far too often.

The Rebel Lawyer

Perhaps Accuser-Adversary's original job was to test the faithfulness of people who called themselves Christians, and if they proved false or hypocritical, to fair-mindedly accuse them before the court of heaven and let God be the judge. If so, the healthiest and most accurate way to view the devil is as a formerly righteous, now-evil tester-tempter called Accuser-Adversary. It is perhaps most helpful to picture Accuser-Adversary originally employed as the zealously patriotic attorney general of heaven and earth, a sort of spiritual Interpol agent meets Hague International Court of Justice prosecutor tasked with carefully and judiciously testing the integrity of all those who dared to claim citizenship to such a lofty kingdom, but who later yearned for the position of King and Judge himself.

The Greek word for a test is *peirasmos* and it appears twenty-one times in the New Testament. The word can mean both a test or a temptation, and depending on the context, sometimes both at the same time. A related Greek word is *peirazó*, to test or tempt, which occurs thirty-nine times and also has the flexible dual meaning. Typically, the test is the positive side of the coin, and the temptation is the negative side. A test is an invitation to faithfulness, whereas a temptation is a lure to sin. Take a guess which way Accuser-Adversary leans. When Jesus is led by the Spirit into the wilderness in Matthew 4:1, He's off to be "tempted by the devil." God, on the other hand, never tempts us to do evil. James 1:13 says: "Let no one say when he is tempted, 'I am being tempted by God,' for God cannot be tempted with evil, and he himself tempts no one." When Jesus prays, "lead us not into temptation," he's asking God to spare us from Accuser-Adversary's attempts to twist a righteous test into an opportunity for rebellion.

What if the Accuser-Adversary's original role as tester wasn't to provoke, torture, discourage, or even tempt Christians, but to help prepare them for victory and glory by acting as a member of the Christian Refinement Committee? What if he overstepped his authority and is now working well outside his mandate? Instead of testing, he practices tempting. Instead of remaining objective, he hates humanity, conducting his business adversarially instead of fairly, impartially, and judiciously. Rather than simply uncovering and reporting sin, he acts as an agent provocateur to induce people to sin by practicing entrapment. Instead of submitting truthful accusations, he brings false charges. Revelation 12:10 says he accuses Christians "day and night" before God. His new practice is straight-up defamation of Christian character. He works not for justice but from malice. The technical term for this is prosecutorial misconduct, a form of perjury that can be a felony punishable with jail time. No wonder the Bible calls him a slanderer. Remember, God is a God of justice but He's ultimately the God of love. Justice that doesn't serve love is satanic. Accuser-Adversary is a merciless legalist, a fundamentalist extremist who opposes grace. An obsession for justice often signals a deeper motive—for retribution, or a sort of sadomasochistic pleasure in the pain and punishment of perpetrators. Basketball coaches test their star athletes, but they don't try to deceive them. Good teachers test their students, but they don't try to torture them. It is one thing to test or even tempt with righteous motive, but it is another thing to lie and deceive and falsely accuse. Above all, Accuser-Adversary crosses the line in wanting to play King and Judge himself.

The Devil Speaks

"The Devil is a better theologian than any of us and is a devil still."

—A.W. Tozer

Considering Accuser-Adversary fancies himself the sovereign of this world and the main player in human history, he gets fewer lines in the Bible than the twelfth lead in an off-Broadway play. In fact, Accuser-Adversary speaks on just five occasions in the entire Bible (Job 1:7, 9–11; Job 2:2, 4–5; Matthew 4:3, 6, 9; Luke 4:3, 6–7, 9–11; and Genesis 3:1, 4–5 if the serpent is Accuser-Adversary). Out of sixty-six books in Scripture, the devil utters a mere eighteen sentences across only four of those books. Seven of his sentences are either quotes or misquotes of Bible verses, and in five of his lines he is just repeating himself. When you eliminate the repeats, he speaks a maximum of just 230 English words, a trifling 0.03 percent of the Bible's total ESV word count. Accuser-Adversary's verbal contribution to Scripture equates to essentially rounding error.

There is much to learn from what little Accuser-Adversary has to say, though.

First, it is clear that he can speak to God.

Second, he can speak to humans, though perhaps not audibly.

Third, it's clear he's active in heaven and on earth and that his work is limited to his role as tester and accuser.

Fourth, he knows his Bible and knows it well enough to twist it better than any televangelist, medieval warlord, or jungle cult guru. Let's camp on this last point for a second. In Matthew 4 and elsewhere, Accuser-Adversary pits verse against verse and goes shot for shot in using the Bible to try to induce Jesus to sin. How wild is that? If one of the devil's tactics with Jesus is to twist Scripture, we should absolutely assume he'll do the same thing with us—and also use humans to twist Scripture for sinful ends. That's why Paul tells his young disciple in 1 Timothy 4:16, "Keep a close watch on yourself and on the teaching. Persist in this, for by so doing you will save both yourself and your hearers." This is an affirmation of Proverbs 4:13, "Keep hold of instruction; do not let go; guard her, for she is your life."

———

There is good news in all this rebellion: Accuser-Adversary does *not* have carte blanche to test Christians. The scope of his reach and power is never outside the allowance of God's will. That's not to say Accuser-Adversary can't occasionally get permission to seriously mess with people's lives. With permission he can:

1. Cause physical ailments (2 Corinthians 12:7; Acts 10:38).
2. Block apostles from taking a missionary trip (1 Thessalonians 2:18).
3. Inspire churchgoers to commit financial fraud (Acts 5:3).
4. Get a disciple to rebuke Jesus (Mark 8:33).
5. Inspire evil authorities to lock up Christians (Revelation 2:10).
6. Incite an apostle to be party to a murder (John 13:2).
7. Inspire false apostles to masquerade as Christians (2 Corinthians 11:13–15).
8. Sift apostles and disciples (Luke 22:31–32).
9. Put his spirit to work in non-Christians (Ephesians 2:2).

Only in extreme instances does Accuser-Adversary gain permission to excuse himself from heaven's court to personally indwell a human being (possibly the King of Tyre in Ezekiel 28:11–19, Judas in John 13:27/Luke 22:3, potentially the Antichrist in 2 Thessalonians 2:3–12, and potentially the false prophet in Revelation 13:11–18).

Accuser-Adversary's powers are seriously curtailed by God, and it appears the devil is not ever allowed to act independently of God.

1. He cannot afflict Job without permission (Job 1:12), and he is expressly forbidden from killing him (Job 2:6–7).

2. He can't perform genuine miracles, though he's quite adept at trickery and false signs (2 Thessalonians 2:9–10; Revelation 13:13–14).

3. He has zero control over human free will and can't force anyone to sin (James 1:14–15).

4. He cannot overpower Christians with unbearable or inescapable temptations (1 Corinthians 10:13).

5. There's nothing in Scripture that says Accuser-Adversary can read minds. But he's had millennia of observation, so let's assume he has expert knowledge of how to manipulate the human psyche, and I have no doubt that he and his angels weaponize group mesmerism, mob mentality, collective mania, and every other psychological technique they've picked up in the past 6,000-plus years of human manipulation.

6. Accuser-Adversary also doesn't seem to have the ability to create anything. As far as we know, the devil can't conjure up a single quark, gluon, or atom, let alone a solar system, galaxy cluster, or universe.

7. Evil people are often described as "the devil incarnate," but Accuser-Adversary is a spirit, and nothing in Scripture suggests he can incarnate in a physical body. He does not have a beating heart, breathing lungs, and a working spleen. All descriptions of him seem symbolic or metaphoric, and even when he does appear, it's in the appearance of a dragon or serpent or what have you. Accuser-Adversary has powers, perhaps even apparitional powers, but these powers are exercised solely within the limits of God's sovereignty and as part of God's ultimate purpose.

8. He cannot keep Christians in habitual sin, nor can he destroy or capture a Christian soul (1 John 5:18–19).

9. He cannot prevail against the truth that Jesus is the Christ and the Son of God (Matthew 16:15–18).

10. He cannot separate Christians from the love of God (Romans 8:31–39).

11. He cannot escape his fate (Revelation 20).

Unlike God, Accuser-Adversary isn't omnipresent (Job 1:7) even though he's a deceiver who'd like you to believe otherwise (Revelation 12:9). There is nothing in Scripture that suggests he is an omnipresent being, that is, that he can be multiple places at the same time. Because he can't be everywhere at once, he has to travel from place to place like any other spirit. If you do the math, in a world with eight billion people, over the course of a century Accuser-Adversary could only spend 0.39 seconds with each of us. In all likelihood, most humans will go their entire lives without ever encountering the devil at all.

It is my strong hunch that Accuser-Adversary spends most of his limited time trying to douse on-fire Christians. In the few times he does crop up in the Bible, it's mostly to harass lovers of God (especially Jesus and His prophets and apostles). As Martin Luther put it in *Colloquia Mensalia*, "For, where God built a church, there the devil would also build a chapel."[2] That said, millions of churchgoers believe Accuser-Adversary is tempting and terrorizing them every day without fail, but it's exceedingly unlikely that the average person will ever have a personal run-in with him in their entire lives. That is not to say they will not encounter the lies, accusations, and life-destroying systems he has been designing and detonating in human hearts since the beginning of time. In World War II, 99.99 percent of the Allies never came face-to-face with Adolf Hitler, but they encountered his lies and allies from Belgium to North Africa and we're still digging up bombs planted by Nazis eighty years ago. In the same way, you can't walk ten feet without encountering a dozen of Accuser-Adversary's schemes, in everything from shopping addiction to low-interest loans to the promise of viral Internet fame.

So long as people sit harmlessly in church and never really act like Jesus—spreading the good news of the kingdom of God, giving until poverty is eradicated, speaking truth to power no matter the cost, actively loving our enemies—Accuser-Adversary appears happy to let us warm the pews. Even the unbelieving world is baffled by how comfortable and complacent millions of our churches have become compared with the poverty and suffering and corruption that surrounds their church buildings.

Accuser-Adversary is powerful, but the good news is that Christians are also given powers with which to fight back. At various times and places, God has given Christians the ability to:

1. Heal the sick (Luke 10:9).
2. Subject demons to the name of Jesus (Luke 10:17).
3. Cast out demons and speak in new languages (Mark 16:17).
4. Drink poison and not die (Mark 16:18).
5. No longer be slaves to sin (Romans 6:14).
6. Overcome sin and temptation and live righteously (Romans 8:13).
7. Be anxious about nothing (Philippians 4:4–7).
8. Abound in hope (Romans 15:13).
9. Directly ask God for wisdom (James 1:5).
10. Interpret spiritual truths (1 Corinthians 2:12–16).
11. Extinguish the flaming darts of the evil one (Ephesians 6:16).
12. Resist the devil until he flees (James 4:7).
13. Overcome the world (1 John 5:4–5; John 16:33).

Accuser-Adversary has limited power, we have opposing power, and God is all-powerful. The reality is that all of Accuser-Adversary's temptations are resistible. First Corinthians 10:13 says, "No temptation has overtaken you that is not common to man. God is faithful, and he will not let you be tempted beyond your ability, but with the temptation he will also provide the way of escape, that you may be able to endure it." This is a hard word to swallow. Not a single temptation you and I have ever faced couldn't have been overcome with God's help. All the cross words toward our spouse, all the impatient moments with our kids, all the hurtful and unkind things we said in anger, all the lust, jealousy, gossip, drunkenness, gluttony, and unforgiveness . . . all of it was escapable. When we said yes to temptation, we said yes to sin. There is not a single excuse in the universe for rape, murder, or turning a profit off the poor. Our response to the truth about all temptation being overcome-able should embolden us to flee from the worship of all idols (1 Corinthians 10:14).

8

HOW TO RESIST THE DEVIL

"We gain the strength of the temptation we resist."

—Ralph Waldo Emerson, *The Conduct of Life*

WHEN I TOLD MY FRIEND Ray Paul (the elder emeritus of our church) that I was writing a book on Accuser-Adversary, he wrote back 2 Corinthians 2:11 in the King James Version: "Lest Satan should get an advantage of us: for we are not ignorant of his devices." No, Accuser-Adversary does not have digital devices like tablets or mobile phones—though much of social media and all of porn is certainly demonic and satanic.

My Finnish father-in-law, Ari, is a renowned trapper of squirrels. Adorable though they may seem, the furry rodents are destroying the half-century-old maple tree in Ari's back yard. So, Ari sets live traps. When he catches his would-be tree-fellers, he does what is perhaps the most humane and over-generous thing possible: He drives across town and releases them in the wild . . . in an arboretum.

Setting traps has a huge advantage for the trapper. Ari doesn't actually have to remain present to nab his prey. In the same way, Accuser-Adversary has set traps all over the world. Some of his devices are significantly more complex and dastardly than a humane live trap, and are more akin to a bear trap or a guillotine.

In his 1652 book *Precious Remedies Against Satan's Devices*, the Puritan preacher Thomas Brooks compiles a lengthy inventory of the devil's devices, and below thirty-eight are presented. It's been nearly 400 years since Brooks penned his list, and it's remarkable to see how strangely modern and relevant Accuser-Adversary's tactics still are.[1]

Accuser-Adversary's devices to draw the soul to sin:

1. To present the bait and hide the hook.
2. To paint sin with virtue's colors.
3. To extenuate and lessen sin.
4. To show the saint his sins, but hide his graces.
5. To present God to the soul as one made up of all mercy.
6. To present the soul with the best men's sins.
7. To make the soul bold to venture upon the occasions of sin.
8. To make the soul believe that repentance is easy and that therefore he can sin now and repent later.
9. To cause the soul to compare his sins with those reputed worse than himself.
10. To make the soul weary of waiting for God's help.
11. To make the soul look more at the trouble than at the end of the trouble.
12. To make the soul ignorant of its own ability to resist sin.

Accuser-Adversary's devices to keep the soul from holy duties:

13. By presenting the world in such a dress as to ensnare the soul.

14. By presenting to the soul the dangers and troubles that attend the performance of holy duties and services.

15. By presenting to the soul the difficulty of performing religious duties.

16. By causing the soul to draw false inferences from the blessed and glorious things that Christ has done.

17. By presenting to view the fewness and poverty of those who hold to religious practices.

18. By showing saints that their labors are in vain, and that they shall never attain their end by their religious duties.

19. By making saints think that their religious performances are hypocritical and not accepted by God.

20. By making saints think that God is weary of them and their religious duties.

Accuser-Adversary's devices to keep saints in a sad, doubting, questioning, and uncomfortable condition:

21. By causing saints to be still poring and musing upon sin, to mind their sins more than their Savior, yes, so to mind their sins as to forget and neglect their Savior.

22. By causing saints to make false definitions of their graces, and false inferences from the cross actings of their graces.

23. By suggesting to saints that their graces are not true, but counterfeit.

24. By suggesting to saints that they have no graces at all, because they have no assurance of them.

25. By persuading saints that their state is not good now, nor ever shall be better hereafter.

26. By reminding saints of their frequent relapses into sin previously prayed over, repented of, and resolved against.

Accuser-Adversary's devices to destroy and ensnare all sorts and ranks of men in the world:

27. To ensnare children by stirring up parents' hearts to neglect their duty toward them, or by stirring up children's hearts to despise their parents' authority over them.

28. To ensnare servants by stirring up masters' hearts either not to provide for them what is fitting or not to correct them with wisdom and gentleness; or by stirring up servants' hearts either not to be diligent in their work or not to be respectful and obedient to their masters.

29. To ensnare wives by stirring up husbands' hearts either not to love them as they should or not to deal with them wisely and tenderly; or by stirring up wives' hearts either not to submit themselves as they should or not to seek their husbands' good as they should.

30. To ensnare husbands by stirring up wives' hearts either not to be prudent in managing household affairs or not to be chaste in preserving their honor; or by stirring up husbands' hearts either not to be faithful in keeping their marriage covenant or not to be content with what God has given them.

31. To ensnare ministers by stirring up people's hearts either not to honor them as they should or not to support them as they should; or by stirring up ministers' hearts either not to preach sound doctrine as they should or not to live holy lives as they should.

32. To ensnare people by stirring up magistrates' hearts either not to execute justice as they should or not to show mercy as they should; or by stirring up people's hearts either not to obey magistrates as they should or not to pray for magistrates as they should.

33. To ensnare learned men by stirring up scholars' hearts either not to acknowledge God as they should or not to use their learning for God's glory as they should; or by stirring up ignorant men's hearts either not to value learning as they should or not to seek learning as they should.

34. To ensnare rich men by stirring up wealthy men's hearts either not to trust in God as they should or not to use their riches for God's service as they should; or by stirring up poor men's hearts either not to be content with what God has given them or not to work hard for what God has appointed them.

35. To ensnare young men by stirring up youths' hearts either not to remember their Creator as they should or not to restrain their passions as they should; or by stirring up old men's hearts either not to be sober and watchful as they should or not to be fruitful and useful as they should.

36. To ensnare all sorts of men by stirring up their hearts either not to believe in God as they should or not to fear God as they should; or by stirring up their hearts either not to love God as they should or not to serve God as they should.

37. To ensnare all sorts of men by stirring up their hearts either not to pray to God as they should or not to praise God as they should; or by stirring up their hearts either not to depend on God as they should or not to delight in God as they should.

38. To ensnare all sorts of men by stirring up their hearts either not to be humble before God as they should or not to be thankful to God as they should; or by stirring up their hearts either not to be patient under God's hand as they should or not to be obedient to God's will as they should.

How convicting is that list? How many of these devices have you experienced? I went nearly thirty-eight for thirty-eight.

What is the common thread across all of these devices? They're all based on lies. Which makes sense, because Accuser-Adversary is an inveterate liar. Evidently, he was the first being in history to practice lying because Jesus calls him the original fibber in John 8:44: Accuser-Adversary "does not stand in the truth, because there is no truth in him. When he lies, he speaks out of his own character, for he is a liar and the father of lies."

Accuser-Adversary's list of lies runs longer than the *Lord of the Rings* fan credits. In his book *God's Devil*, Erwin Lutzer lists a litany of lies that Accuser-Adversary has been using and refining for millennia.[2]

1. Accuser-Adversary lies about who God is, by planting questions that produce distrust instead of faith. It starts all the way back in Genesis 3:1 with "Did God actually say, 'You shall not eat of any tree in the garden'?" Churchgoers fall for this line of question *all the time.*

   With money: *Did God actually say don't charge interest, or can we pretend usury has a different definition?*

   With politics: *Did God really say love your enemies and turn the other cheek or can we practice mutually assured destruction?*

   With sexuality: *Did God really say people can't have sex before marriage or is it okay because we're planning to get married anyway?*

   We play the "Did God actually say" game with drunkenness, violence, power, amassing wealth, overeating, and a thousand other things. A few years ago in Canada, where I grew up, hundreds of members of Parliament rose in a standing ovation for the "moral" right to murder unborn babies. Accuser-Adversary loves to twist and pervert the world until everything is upside-down and wrong seems right (Isaiah 5:20). The deceiver's worldview is so bent that he even has the gall to accuse God of deception. The father of lies claims God is untruthful.

2. Accuser-Adversary lies about who he is by pretending he is ultimate when he's entirely subordinate. This extends to his temptations too. Idolatry is making anything subordinate ultimate. Think of how many political parties in history have tried to subordinate Christianity to their political purposes. The party was everything to them. Think of how many economic systems claim the Bible is on "their side." When God becomes anything less than Number One, we make Him zero. Jesus says to seek first His kingdom and His righteousness. If faith in Christ is only acceptable if we first adopt the world's beliefs on sex or gender or social justice or abortion or any other issue, then the true gods of the age are revealed.

Accuser-Adversary wants to deceive us into believing that a part is the whole. That technology is everything. That expressing our identity is the key to fulfillment. That progress is the highest aim. That corporate rights and shareholder profits are sacrosanct. That money or power or fame or racial emancipation is the savior. Every day we face false gospels that claim to be ultimate and the whole, when they are all subordinate and only a tiny part.

3. Accuser-Adversary lies about who we are. He tries to delude us into believing that we are autonomous, sovereign, and ultimate. That we are better than we are. That we are less than we are. That we are in his debt or power. Above all, he tries to convince us that we have the final say on what is right and wrong.

4. Accuser-Adversary lies about what he can do for us. The devil is the seed oil margarine to God's grass-fed butter. Accuser-Adversary gives us what we want, not what we need.

5. Accuser-Adversary lies about the benefits of sin. His promise often takes the form of a bait and switch. At first, rebellion delivers a big benefit and costs nearly nothing, but eventually

it requires everything and delivers nothing. I can think of no better example of this than pornography. When I directed the documentary *Over 18*, we met countless men who discovered porn as children. At first, it was a huge rush of buzzy brain chemicals with no physical downsides. But over time, as their addiction grew worse, porn delivered a small hit at a much greater price—the cost of parental relationships, sibling relationships, friendships with the opposite sex, broken marriages, and zombie-like emotional numbness. For the men I've met who descended into child pornography, the cost included social stigma and jail time, not to mention the horrific effects on the victims. Tens of thousands of young men are also experiencing porn-induced erectile dysfunction—porn promised better sex, but in the end, these men can't even have sex with a real woman because their brains only respond to digital stimulus. Accuser-Adversary sells sin for its short term "benefits," while trying to lock us into a lifelong contract with compounding prices and ever-diminishing returns. Romans 6:23 is right: On the eternal time scale, the wages of sin are literally death.

6. Accuser-Adversary lies about the nature of reality. The first lie ever recorded was the biggest lie in the universe: That creatures can be like the Creator in defining good and evil. That a temporary being knows better than Being himself. All other lies descend from this colossal original lie.

In addition to Accuser-Adversary's perspective-based lies, Erwin Lutzer also outlines Accuser-Adversary's arsenal of lies about how we can become like God.[3]

1. The lie of immortality
     In Genesis 3:4, the serpent promises Adam and Eve that they will not die. Today, Silicon Valley venture capitalists promise us everything from tech-based longevity and cloning

to AI-driven afterlives. From cryogenic brain freezing to neural-linked brain implants, there's massive money to be made in pretending humans can live forever as they would like to. For the ultra-rich in times past, it was leaving colossal monuments, towers, temples, and pyramids. For some (myself included), the temptation to immortality lies in leaving a literary legacy. For power-seekers, political immortality can be a main driver for holding on to public office. For artists, it's leaving behind a great work of art. For musicians, it's a hit song. For actors, it's an image on the silver screen. For teenagers, it's going viral on social media. Humans will live forever, but it won't be by any of the means we're currently chasing. Immortality belongs to God, and He sets the terms.

2. The lie of works

In Genesis 3:7, after Adam and Eve have sinned, they try to hide their guilt and exposed bodies by working to sew fig leaves into coverings. Accuser-Adversary would have us believe the only way to get into heaven is through good works. Being nice gets us rewarded, being bad gets us punished. Think karma. Think Catholic indulgences. Think Hinduism with its dehumanizing caste system. Muslims, Hindus, many Catholics, and millions of Protestants are wrong—there is nothing we can do to warrant entry into heaven. Our best efforts are like filthy rags (Isaiah 64:6). We cannot cover our exposure with work. Quite incredibly, some key biblical images of salvation involve God clothing us with His righteousness even though we deserve none of it (Zechariah 3:1–4; Revelation 19:6–8; Isaiah 61:10).

3. The lie of enlightenment

In Genesis 3:5, the serpent promises to open Adam and Eve's eyes to all knowledge. Isn't that the promise of today's technocrats? Given enough time and technology—namely, a brain implant attached to an ever-growing Internet—humans can become all-knowing. But knowledge without wisdom is dangerous. Knowledge without wisdom is what created the atomic bomb that killed more than 100,000 Japanese civilians. Knowledge without wisdom is evident in IBM designing the technology used to track millions of Jewish prisoners in concentration camps.* It was knowledge without wisdom that created the thumbscrew, the iron maiden, the Catherine wheel, the Brazen bull, the Judas cradle, the rack, and the crucifixion cross. All technologies have their costs and benefits, but what will be said of artificial intelligence a century from now? First Corinthians 3:19 says "the wisdom of this world is folly with God," and James 3:13–18 calls this sort of "wisdom" demonic.

4. The lie of godhood

In Genesis 3:5, the serpent does not confine the promise of Adam and Eve becoming like God to being all-knowing. Brain-web implants promise omnipresence, the ability to be online and connected, to be everything everywhere all at once. Omnipotence is also on offer, with technologies like the Large Hadron Collider, nuclear fusion, and space travel promising humans will eventually become all-powerful. Scientific experimentation and discovery are wonderful when animated by the righteous motives of earlier discoverers like Copernicus, Galileo, Newton, and Kepler, but these curious men were driven by a will to life and worship, not to personal profit and power.

5. The lie of relativism

Also in Genesis 3:5, the serpent promises Adam and Eve the ability to define good and evil on their own terms. But how could non-infinite, non-omniscient, non-omnipotent, non-omnipresent, deeply imperfect humans possibly know what is perfectly and ultimately good in a universe containing unlimited variables? It is impossible. (We'll attack relativism ferociously in chapter 9, so stay tuned.)

---

* For more on this, see historian Edwin Black's book *IBM and the Holocaust*.

6. The lie of pleasure

In Genesis 3:6, the woman (she's not named Eve for another fourteen verses) saw the fruit and it looked good. The lie of pleasure tells us never to think, ponder, or deliberate, just to *feel*. If it feels good, do it. Hedonism is the belief that personal happiness is the ultimate good. But what happens when one person's happiness causes or even requires someone else's pain? Plus, as we've seen, pleasure promises much but eventually delivers nothing while costing everything.

7. The lie of spirituality

Accuser-Adversary wants you to believe you can have a religious experience without religion. He wants us to worship, but without an object of worship. "Oneness" is a major player here, with the notion that God is everything and everything is God. The trope of smoking peyote and wandering Joshua Tree National Park in search of a vision or engaging in the nonmedical use of psychedelics are textbook examples of seeking spirituality without the Holy Spirit.

We've now covered Accuser-Adversary's devices and major lies. Next, we'll see how he manages to wiggle a foot into our lives before storming the castle and making it his fortress.

Footholds and Strongholds

A spiritual foothold occurs when someone allows Accuser-Adversary the opportunity to jam his foot in the door of their life. The original Greek word for opportunity (*topos*) is sometimes translated into English as "foothold." Ephesians 4:27 in the NIV says, "Do not give the devil a foothold." If we don't shut sin out and refuse to let it enter, but instead leave Accuser-Adversary with a foot in the door, it appears he simply uses the opening to lob grenades through the crack until he eventually blasts his way in. Once inside, he tries to set up permanent shop. A stronghold is simply that—a strong hold. A stronghold is a sin that metastasizes into a powerful habit. Let's look at a few examples.

Foothold: **Self-will**
Stronghold: **Disobedience and rebellion**

The root of all sin is the self-will that says "I want" instead of "Your will be done." The foothold of self-will eventually grows into the refusal to submit to God and all God-permitted authorities, including parents, spouses, church elders, and even the government and masters.[*]

Foothold: **Anger**
Stronghold: **Violence**

All technologies have a bent. For instance, nuclear warheads and semiautomatic weapons are more likely to kill people than, say, feather pillows or paperback books. Anger can be as useful as a campfire to heat your coffee while camping, but anger has a bent that makes it more like a forest fire than a kettle warmer. Our anger needs to stay conscious, intentional, redemptive, and incredibly short-lived. Anger itself is not a sin, but the Bible explicitly says anger creates a foothold for Accuser-Adversary. Ephesians 4:26–27 says, "Be angry and do not sin; do not let the sun go down on your anger, and give no opportunity to the devil." Anger doesn't produce the righteousness God desires (James 1:19–20), which is why it's so important to flush it from our system before we go to sleep. Otherwise, compounding anger taken to its fullness inevitably

---

[*] There is, of course, nuance to all human forms of authority. Christians submit to all God-permitted authorities only so far as they submit to Christ, and are willing to suffer the temporary consequences of civil disobedience in their quest to maintain eternal fidelity. The Bible is full of stories of people who disobeyed earthly laws in faithful submission to the laws of heaven. Christians must refuse to obey any law that denies the truth or dehumanizes or hurts others. As Ken Satterfield wrote, "When the king demands blasphemy, breaking the law is faithfulness." ("Jesus Broke the Law. Hallelujah!" *Word & Way*, July 12, 2018). If the English or Nazi powers tell us to hand over the Catholics or the Jews, we hide them or die trying.

leads to violence. That's why Jesus takes the foothold of anger so seriously in Matthew 5:21–22. "You have heard that it was said to those of old, 'You shall not murder; and whoever murders will be liable to judgment.' But I say to you that everyone who is angry with his brother will be liable to judgment; whoever insults his brother will be liable to the council; and whoever says, 'You fool!' will be liable to the hell of fire." The phrase "you fool" is often left untranslated from Jesus's original language, Aramaic. The word *raca* means worthless, empty-headed, or stupid. For Jesus, contempt toward another image-bearer puts us at risk of hellfire.

Foothold: **Hatred**
Stronghold: **Murder**

Hatred and murder are closely related to anger and violence. The first murder in history was caused by the hatred of righteousness. "We should not be like Cain, who was of the evil one and murdered his brother. And why did he murder him? Because his own deeds were evil and his brother's righteous" (1 John 3:12). Jesus in His brilliance is always filling up the Old Testament law with love so the law itself is fulfilled. In Matthew 5:43–45 He says, "You have heard that it was said, 'You shall love your neighbor and hate your enemy.' But I say to you, Love your enemies and pray for those who persecute you, so that you may be sons of your Father who is in heaven." Christians who have crucified their anger and banished hatred from their hearts don't need any of the Old Testament violence and murder laws because they've filled them up with love for brother and enemy alike (Romans 13:8–10).

Foothold: **Unforgiveness**
Stronghold: **Bitterness**

Unforgiveness is risky business. In 2 Corinthians 2:10–11, Paul shows the lengths to which he's willing to go in forgiving those who've wronged him and why. "Anyone whom you forgive, I also forgive. Indeed, what I have forgiven, if I have forgiven anything, has been for your sake in the presence of Christ, so that we would not be outwitted by Satan." Jesus tells Peter to forgive his brother a figurative seventy-seven times (Matthew 18:22). We forgive others because God forgave us (Colossians 3:13). Otherwise, chronic unforgiveness festers into an interior bitterness that poisons relationships, often permanently. Hebrews 12:15 (NIV) warns us, "See to it that no one fails to obtain the grace of God and that no bitter root grows up to cause trouble and defile many." Most terrifyingly of all, God's forgiveness of our sins is conditioned upon our forgiving others (Matthew 6:14–15).

Foothold: **Lust**
Stronghold: **Adultery**

Jesus fills the Old Testament adultery commands with love, too. "You have heard that it was said, 'You shall not commit adultery.' But I say to you that everyone who looks at a woman with lustful intent has already committed adultery with her in his heart" (Matthew 5:27–28). In 1 Corinthians 7:5, Paul offers additional advice for married couples, encouraging them to have sex regularly "so that Satan may not tempt you because of your lack of self-control." I've seen the foothold of lust destroy lives and families. I know multiple men who've given up on marriages because their pornography strongholds were more enticing to them. In the Bible, Job avoided the stronghold and foothold of lust by making a covenant with his eyes never to look lustfully at a woman (Job 31:1). You don't need a law against the stronghold of adultery if you never give lust a foothold.

Foothold: **Guilt**
Stronghold: **Condemnation**

Guilt can be very good and very bad. Guilt can lead to either satanic shame or godly grief. Few things are so life-improving as Christ-centered contrition and righteous sorrow at sin. "Godly grief produces a repentance that leads to salvation without regret, whereas worldly grief produces death" (2 Corinthians 7:10).

Notice how God and Accuser-Adversary use guilt for opposite purposes: Accuser-Adversary uses guilt to drive us into hiding away from the presence of God (think Adam and Eve in the garden of Eden), while the Holy Spirit uses guilt to drive us right back into the arms of the Father who's already forgiven us. The only acceptable "guilt" in a Christian's life is the sense of conviction that comes from the Holy Spirit. Often, righteous judgment is voiced through the church. As Paul wrote in 1 Corinthians 5:9–13,

> I wrote to you in my letter not to associate with sexually immoral people—not at all meaning the sexually immoral of this world, or the greedy and swindlers, or idolaters, since then you would need to go out of the world. But now I am writing to you not to associate with anyone who bears the name of brother if he is guilty of sexual immorality or greed, or is an idolater, reviler, drunkard, or swindler—not even to eat with such a one. For what have I to do with judging outsiders? Is it not those inside the church whom you are to judge? God judges those outside. "Purge the evil person from among you."

There's absolutely a place for holy judgment in the church, but *unholy* guilt leads to the condemnation (and often damnation) of self and others. Don't let yourself slip into burying yourself under a mountain of unproductive guilt. Ignore your head, Accuser-Adversary, and everyone else. "There is therefore now no condemnation for those who are in Christ Jesus. For the law of the Spirit of life has set you free in Christ Jesus from the law of sin and death" (Romans 8:1–2).

In the same way, try not to heap guilt on others.

> You have no excuse, O man, every one of you who judges. For in passing judgment on another you condemn yourself, because you, the judge, practice the very same things. . . . Do you suppose, O

man—you who judge those who practice such things and yet do them yourself—that you will escape the judgment of God? Or do you presume on the riches of his kindness and forbearance and patience, not knowing that God's kindness is meant to lead you to repentance?

Romans 2:1, 3–4

When it comes to guilt, we need to strike a balance between condemnatory fundamentalism and cheap grace.

Foothold: Fear
Stronghold: Paralysis

A good bellwether of faith is how much fear we still harbor in our hearts. Am I afraid of death? Am I afraid of running out of money? Am I afraid of standing up for the truth if it will cost me personally? If you want to know if you've been perfected in God's love, check out 1 John 4:12–13, 18. "If we love one another, God abides in us and his love is perfected in us. By this we know that we abide in him and he in us, because he has given us of his Spirit. . . . There is no fear in love, but perfect love casts out fear. For fear has to do with punishment, and whoever fears has not been perfected in love." Fear paralyses. Trust releases. "God gave us a spirit not of fear but of power and love and self-control" (2 Timothy 1:7). He will strengthen, uphold, and protect us from letting a foothold of fear become a stronghold of paralysis (Isaiah 41:10).

Foothold: Distraction
Stronghold: Idol worship

At its core, worship is attention. Whatever gets the majority of our time, energy, mental bandwidth, and emotion is the thing we worship.

The challenge for us is that our worship is so well diversified. We do church on Sundays, plus maybe midweek small group and daily devotions, but then we've got our favorite shows, sport teams, social media apps, influencers, politicians, musicians, movie stars, friends, heroes, enemies, and kids, not to mention our car, clothes, devices, house, and retirement portfolio. Our gods are many, so they don't seem to be bigger than God. But what would happen if we added up all the little gods that vie for our worship? If we melted them all down into one big god, how much larger would its shadow loom over our lives compared with God's?

Idol worship is a big deal in the Bible. As the Israelites enter the Promised Land, God specifically tells them not to worship idols like the locals, some of whom were even burning their children alive as offerings to their gods (Deuteronomy 18:9–10). Today's Christian parent might not be immolating their children, but millions of them have forfeited their children's discipleship in the way of Christ. I've seen the foothold of distraction choke out the faith of hundreds of teenagers. Smartphones are addiction devices for changing people's behaviors, and kids are even more impressionable than their parents and grandparents. It's no accident that teens around the world can be spotted literally bowing their heads—that little screen is a spiritual formation machine that is teaching our children they are the center of the universe, and that every second of boredom, lust, fear, and curiosity can and should be instantly fulfilled without any effort, sacrifice, or relationship. I'm not saying we should say to our teens, "Thou shalt not have a cell phone." I'm saying we should all read 1 Corinthians 6:12—"'All things are lawful for me,' but not all things are helpful. 'All things are lawful for me,' but I will not be dominated by anything."

Foothold: Conceit
Stronghold: Pride

Haughtiness goes before an inevitable fall, and pride is a precursor to destruction (Proverbs 16:18). God actively opposes the proud (James 4:6), which is probably why Paul warns Timothy that new converts shouldn't be selected as church overseers because they "may become puffed up with conceit and fall into the condemnation of the devil" (1 Timothy 3:6).

A good indicator of conceit is thinking you're smart (Proverbs 26:12). Romans 1:22 says anyone who claims to be wise is a straight-up fool. It's silly to boast because 100 percent of the things we have came from God (1 Corinthians 4:7).

Whether our foothold of conceit is our new electric car, prestigious degree, corner office, washboard abs, or fashionable outfit, 1 Peter 5:5 suggests clothing ourselves with humility so God can send His grace before pride blows up our lives.

Foothold: False teaching
Stronghold: Apostasy

One of Paul's most forceful exhortations is in 1 Timothy 4:1–2. "Now the Spirit expressly says that in later times some will depart from the faith by devoting themselves to deceitful spirits and teachings of demons, through the insincerity of liars whose consciences are seared." Unbiblical teaching is rife in modern churches. In fact, I've visited numerous church services in my travels where the Bible is never even opened. (My favorite was a Unitarian church in New England that read ABBA lyrics.)

One easy way to spot false teaching is that it lacks all feeling of conviction. I once was the guest preacher at a megachurch where the pastor said, "Please don't mention sin. Our goal every week is to make sure people come back next Sunday." If the Sunday teaching you receive is comfortable, it's probably not biblical. If the teaching you receive requires nothing of you, no obedience, surrender, sacrifice, then it's probably false. That said, the opposite can also be true. If it's nothing but fire, hell, brimstone, guilt, judgment, fear, and condemnation, it's probably also false teaching. First Thessalonians 5:21 offers the prettiest little prescription: "Test everything; hold fast what is good." There are so many false prophets in the world that 1 John 4:1 counsels us to "not believe every spirit, but test the spirits to see whether they are from God." The earliest masters of this practice were the Berean Christians of southwest Macedonia, who in Acts 17:11 "received the word with all eagerness, examining the Scriptures daily to see if these things were so." My father taught me to take nothing at face value. Run it by the Word. Reject what doesn't line up. By slamming the door on the foothold of false teaching, we never make space for a stronghold of heresy and then apostasy to form and eventually evict us from the household of faith.

There's good news when it comes to the foothold-stronghold battles we face: We can let God be our stronghold and let Him smash all other strongholds. Psalm 18:2 says, "The LORD is my rock and my fortress and my deliverer, my God, my rock, in whom I take refuge, my shield, and the horn of my salvation, my stronghold." Second Corinthians 10:3–4 says, "For though we walk in the flesh, we are not waging war according to the flesh. For the weapons of our warfare are not of the flesh but have divine power to destroy strongholds."

The key with all these strongholds is to never let sin gain a foothold in the first place.

Next, we'll discover how Accuser-Adversary seeks to entrap us.

Entrapment

Accuser-Adversary seems to have three stages of entrapment:

1. **Temptation:** A desire is introduced. In most cases, it seems simultaneously seductive and innocuous.
2. **Fixation:** An obsession begins to form. We must have the object of our desire. We obsess over it. We crave it.
3. **Possession:** We reach out and snatch it. Once we take possession, we hoard and hide it jealously like a dragon on a pile of gold.

An archetypal depiction of the Temptation-Fixation-Possession trap is the story of Gollum in *Lord of the Rings*. Sméagol desires Déagol's ring. He fixates and obsesses and insists on receiving it for his birthday. He soon reaches out, grasps his friend by the throat, and strangles the life out of him. Now in possession of the ring, he is driven mad by it. His character changes (and so does his name) from a happy hobbit to a cave-dwelling demon of darkness.

The ring is any sinful desire. We find ourselves tempted and fixated. Then, when we do possess the object of our desire, we get possessive. We hoard our wealth. We protect our drinking time. We try to drive a wedge between our best friend and our friend group so we can have both to ourselves. This hideous possessiveness is often displayed by teenage boys when they land their first girlfriend. It also crops up in boardrooms when jockeying for promotions and in political chambers when seeking glory at the passing of legislation. Ironically, the sin we so desperately seek to possess ends up possessing us. We spend our weekends working overtime to pay for, maintain, and clean our oversized houses. We shoulder decades of student debt for a piece of paper with a slightly more prestigious brand name on it. We miss out on a real world of challenge and adventure and triumph because we're addicted to the video-game version.

What's the big deal with sin, anyway? How, exactly, does sin destroy lives? Jesus's brother James tries to answer these questions in his letter to the Jews scattered among the nations. "Each person is tempted when he is lured and enticed by his own desire. Then desire when it has conceived gives birth to sin, and sin when it is fully grown brings forth death" (James 1:14–5).

Sure, you can look at porn once or lie to your spouse once or occasionally drink more than your brain and liver can handle, but sin compounds faster than credit card debt. Sin is like radiation poisoning—left untreated by Christ's holiness in us, the poison will slowly but surely spread until it destroys both body and spirit.

A large portion of growing our faith is coming to believe that sin is as evil as God says it is.

As James suggests, desire is the problem. But Christians don't go after desire in the Buddhist sense. We're not trying to purge all desire until we end up driverless and empty inside. (And ironically, the desire for non-desire is a desire.) The trick, then, is to learn to desire what God desires and despise what God despises. A good gauge of our holiness trajectory is to see if we have a growing hatred, disgust, and revulsion toward the sins in our lives. One of the prayers on my daily list is "God, change my desires! Help me to hate my sin."

There are sinful desires and there are godly desires. James is talking about the former, not the latter. A conceived desire for Christ's presence does not give birth to sin and does not blossom into death. But a conceived desire for personal happiness and hyper-individual autonomy definitely sets our sail in that direction.

The same concept applies to Paul's words in Philippians 2:3. "Do nothing from selfish ambition." Sadly, many churches don't know what to do with attendees who have strong senses of their kingdom calling and a fiery drive to pursue good works. Millions of churchgoers have taken a vague or even negative view of ambition because of this text, but they're focusing on the wrong word in the sentence. It's the *selfishness* that Paul wants to root out of the Christians at Philippi. The Greek word for ambition here is *eritheia*, which roughly means "self-seeking" work. It's mentioned seven times in the New Testament and it's negative every time. But ambition itself isn't the problem. Me-centered ambition is the problem. Shouldn't Christians be the most selflessly ambitious people in the world? Shouldn't we make it our aim to be kingdomly ambitious? We should be ambitious to destroy human trafficking, ambitious to end war, ambitious to rebuild Christian economic systems that eradicate poverty. The world will pay attention when Christians begin to work for the will of God with the empowerment of the Holy Spirit in the name of Jesus.

There are two contrasting ways to live: In the flesh or in the spirit.

Sinful desire → sin → death
Holy desire → righteousness → the life that is truly life

If we understand Accuser-Adversary's devices and are well-versed in his lies, and understand how footholds and strongholds work, and are keenly conscious of the three stages of entrapment, we can let the Holy Spirit reverse engineer a game plan to keep us from sinning.

If we don't want Accuser-Adversary to grow strongholds of sin habits in our lives, then we need to avoid footholds.

To avoid footholds, we need to avoid possession.

To avoid possession, we need to avoid fixation.

To avoid fixation, we need to avoid temptation.

That's why we ask God to lead us away from temptation in the Lord's Prayer. The easiest way to prevent Accuser-Adversary from not growing fortress-like strongholds in our life is to steer ridiculously far from temptation in the first place.

The reason the Titanic sunk wasn't because it hit the iceberg head on. The largest ship in the world sank because it scraped open the starboard hull rather than charting a wide berth around the lethal obstacle. Steering miles clear of temptation is far easier than trying to patch up your sinking life.

Here are some practical examples. It's harder to fall into a stronghold of dairy gluttony if you live fifty miles from the nearest Dairy Queen and don't stock ice cream in your freezer. If you struggle with a shopping addiction, do what we did and move an hour from the nearest mall. It's harder to fall into a stronghold of wealth accumulation if you fire your stockbroker and financial advisor. If drugs have a grip on your body, living in a crack house cannot help. It's significantly easier to not profit off the poor if you sell your stocks and bonds and rental properties. I've never seen porn on a cell phone for the simple reason that I don't own a cell phone. And because I go to bed at the same time as my wife, it prevents me from going on sinful sites late at night when my willpower is weakest.

No opportunity, no temptation, no fixation, no possession, no addiction, no destruction.

But what do we do with the surprise temptations that crop up out of nowhere? First, we thank God. It might seem strange to thank God for temptation, but temptation has a redemptive nature: the opportunity for victory. When tempted, the first thing we should do is thank God for allowing us the opportunity to pass a test. What Accuser-Adversary meant for evil, God meant for good. What Accuser-Adversary meant for temptation, fixation, and addiction, God can redeem as invitation, contestation, and liberation.

If we find ourselves struggling to thank God for any temptation that He allows us to face, it's because we haven't yet discerned our opportunity for growth and victory. That's why prayer—a constant communion with Christ—is our greatest weapon in the fight against temptation. Do you see how brilliant Jesus is? *Even temptation is a servant of God.* Overcoming temptation by the Holy Spirit increases our strength, endurance, perseverance, patience, willpower, discipline, and love for God and others. Who wouldn't want more of these amazing gifts? The word *Satan* becomes Santa by rearranging two letters, and fellow word nerds will appreciate that temptation's anagram is *potent mait*—an Old English term for powerful friend. When entrusted to the Master's hand, temptation becomes a holy tool for sanctification.

After we thank God for allowing us to face temptation, James 4:7 tells Christians, "Submit yourselves therefore to God. Resist the devil, and he will flee from you." Let's note a few things about the text. First, it doesn't say to resist Accuser-Adversary weakly or resist only for a few minutes. It also doesn't say that he'll immediately flee. How, exactly, does one resist temptation, sin, and Accuser-Adversary? I like to think of it as a military battle in three stages.

Stage 1: Armor up

The moment alarm bells sound in a castle to warn of an incoming attack, you don't just run out the front gate in your underwear. You head for the armory, where you suit up for the impending onslaught. Temptation is war, and the stakes are high. A single sin separated mankind from God, and a single sin can cause the death of a stranger, the end of a marriage, the clear-cutting of a rainforest, the crash of a stock market, or the bankruptcy and homelessness of millions. It pays to armor up well in advance of the moment of temptation.

> Finally, be strong in the Lord and in the strength of his might. Put on the whole armor of God, that you may be able to stand against the schemes of the devil. For we do not wrestle against flesh and blood, but against the rulers, against the authorities, against the cosmic powers over this present darkness, against the spiritual forces of evil in the heavenly places. Therefore take up the whole armor of God, that you may be able to withstand in the evil day, and having done all, to stand firm. Stand therefore, having fastened on the belt of truth, and having put on the breastplate of righteousness, and, as shoes for your feet, having put on the readiness given by the gospel of peace. In all circumstances take up the shield of faith, with which you can extinguish all the flaming darts of the evil one; and take the helmet of salvation, and the sword of the Spirit, which is the word of God, praying at all times in the Spirit, with all prayer and supplication.
>
> Ephesians 6:10–18

In case you're wondering, the "flaming darts" in verse sixteen aren't the little spiky bits you'll find at your local sports bar. The better Greek translation here is "flaming missiles." We resist

Accuser-Adversary's darts by armoring ourselves with truth, righteousness, gospel readiness, faith, salvation, the Word of God, and constant prayer.

Stage 2: Be on guard

I live in the United Kingdom, home to some of the best architecture in the world. I'm enchanted by thatched medieval cottages. There are more than 50,000 houses still hatted with thatch, and unbelievably, there are still over 250 roofs in England whose base coats of thatch were applied over 500 years ago; the wheat or rye used for thatching provided straw for the roof and grain for food.[4] God gave our ancestors their daily bread (and beer), along with rainproof shelter for five centuries from the same plant.

The biggest threat to thatched roofs is, of course, fire. A single spark can burn a house to the ground, which is why the owners of thatched homes are vigilant to install chimney flues and fire-resistant under-barriers, sweep the chimney regularly, and coat the thatch with fire-retardant spray. It's also why they don't set off fireworks from their front porch. We should be wary of sin in the same way. Our lives are as brittle and flammable as sunbaked English thatch in July, and a single spark can scorch our lives to cinder.

After getting properly armored, we need to shore up our defenses. Jesus counsels us, "Watch and pray that you may not enter into temptation. The spirit indeed is willing, but the flesh is weak" (Mark 14:38). Peter adds, "Be sober-minded; be watchful. Your adversary the devil prowls around like a roaring lion, seeking someone to devour. Resist him, firm in your faith, knowing that the same kinds of suffering are being experienced by your brotherhood throughout the world" (1 Peter 5:8–9).

It takes armor and rock-solid defenses to stay vigilant against Accuser-Adversary. Many of us were raised to believe that Accuser-Adversary runs away at the mere mention of the name of Jesus or the slightest puff of a prayer. I was taught in Sunday school that all one needed to do to rid a room of demons or the devil was to say "Be gone in Jesus's name." It is a nice thought that Accuser-Adversary flees at the mere mention of Yehoshua ben Yehoseph's English name, but if it were that simple, Christians would have banished him from the continent, Earth, or universe long ago.

Not that keen folks haven't tried. Carolyn Risher, former mayor of Inglis, Florida, made international headlines in 2001 when she signed a civic proclamation officially banning Accuser-Adversary from her town. She said all the "right" words (mentioning Jesus Christ, the blood of the lamb, God of Israel, etc.) and even tucked copies of the proclamation inside hollow fence posts at the four corners of the town—all of which were stolen shortly thereafter.

We must take sin far more seriously. As Thomas Brooks put it in *Precious Remedies Against Satan's Devices*, "He that will play with Satan's bait, will quickly be taken with Satan's hook."[5] It's time to stop toying and start actively resisting. To resist Accuser-Adversary, we must put up a real fight. The Bible describes him as a lion (1 Peter 5:8), disguised as an angel of light (2 Corinthians 11:14), a dragon (Revelation 12:3–4), and a thief (John 10:10). Imagine the amount of resistance it would take to repel any one of these attackers, let alone a being who can act like all four. And even after he flees, Accuser-Adversary simply regroups and comes back—even Paul and Jesus experienced multiple assaults.

Stage 3: Go on the offensive

One of the longest single continuous sieges in history was the Siege of Candia (modern day Heraklion) from 1648 to 1669. Over a miserable span of twenty-one years and four months, 60,000 Muslim Ottomans terrorized the Venetian-governed island of Crete. The Venetians eventually surrendered the keys to the town, led by a rather fabulous doge who only wore red and took his cat into battle with him. It was such a Pyrrhic victory for the attackers that it helped lead to the decline of the Ottoman Empire. One of the Muslim grand viziers, Hezarpare Ahmed Pasha, eventually married a three-year-old girl and was shortly thereafter cut into a thousand pieces by his father-in-law's subjects. That father-in-law, Sultan Ibrahim the Mad, loved raping virgin slaves and overweight women and was himself strangled to death at the behest of his own mother. That mother, Kösem Sultan, was strangled to death a few years later, either by curtain strings or her own braids, possibly at the behest of her own daughter-in-law, Turhan Sultan.

As for Candia and the rest of the island, faithful Christians suffered extreme persecution under their Muslim oppressors for two and a half centuries. When European powers led by Britain eventually intervened to institute civil rights for Christians, Muslim bashi-bazouks ("crazy heads") massacred nearly 1,000 Christians, even burning children alive. That was the straw that broke the camel's back—Queen Victoria personally called for drastic action and the European powers forced the withdrawal of all Muslims from Crete in less than two months.

Sin is a lot like the siege and oppression on Candia. It will hammer at the gates for decades until it gets inside, and then it will cause turmoil and chaos until it kills the host, itself, or both.

Most battles against sin are skirmishes, but sometimes, temptation feels like a decade-long siege. There comes a point when playing defense isn't enough. It's time to make a counterassault and take prisoners. "For though we live in the world, we do not wage war as the world does. The weapons we fight with are not the weapons of the world. On the contrary, they have divine power to demolish strongholds. We demolish arguments and every pretension that sets itself up against the knowledge of God, and we take captive every thought to make it obedient to Christ" (2 Corinthians 10:3–5 NIV).

It really comes down to speaking the truth of Scripture. We must call sin a sin. We must call our rebellion rebellion.

There's more to James 4:7 than I previously shared. "*Submit yourselves therefore to God. Resist the devil, and he will flee* from you" (emphasis added). We can't exercise God's authority until we are *under* His authority. The Word of God must take preeminence. Remember what happens when we try to assert God's authority without being under God's authority: We get brutally exposed. Consider the terrifying story in Acts 19:11–20 about the offspring of a Jewish priest named Sceva. God had been using the apostle Paul to do all sorts of wild miracles including healings and exorcisms via aprons and handkerchiefs (v. 12), and Sceva's seven sons wanted to get in on the action. So they went around trying to cast out demons using the phrase "I adjure you by the Jesus whom Paul proclaims." But one of the evil spirits barks back: "Jesus I know, and Paul I recognize, but who are you?" Things get truly scary for the priest's sons in verse 16: "The man in whom was the evil spirit leaped on them, mastered all of them and overpowered them, so that they fled out of that house naked and wounded."

Make no mistake, friends, we are at war, and the enemy is strong enough to use one person to overpower seven. The only way to win this war is to stay obedient to our commanding officer. The Bible is the sword of truth. The truth is the weapon with which we go on the offensive. It is the Christian's job to stab and slash at lies with the sword of truth. We'll end this chapter with a relevant quote from Timothy Keller in his book *Encounters with Jesus*: "Satan doesn't control us with fang marks on the flesh but with lies in the heart. . . . Our best defense in the fight against . . . lies is generally not the production of incantations but the rehearsal of truth."[6]

PART IV
REDEMPTION

9

THE REASON FOR EVIL

"Poor God, how often He is blamed for all the suffering in the world.
It's like praising Satan for allowing all the good that happens."

—E. A. Bucchianeri, *Brushstrokes of a Gadfly*

THERE IS AN UNDENIABLE PROBLEM in this world. Most people call it evil. There are a few clinically psychopathic anti-theists out there who really believe there's no such thing as evil and that the torture and murder of children is just the amoral rearrangement of molecules, but even the majority of runabout atheists agree bad things happen on planet Earth. Where did evil come from? Why doesn't God stop evil from happening? How could an all-loving and all-powerful God allow evil things to happen to innocent people?

The technical term for this challenge is the *theodicy problem*. It was the eighteenth-century Scottish philosopher David Hume who popularized in his *Dialogues Concerning Natural Religion* what is now known as the problem of evil: "Is he willing to prevent evil, but not able? then is he impotent. Is he able, but not willing? then is he malevolent. Is he both able and willing? whence then is evil?"[1] These are good and important questions . . . when asked in good faith.

To update the language for modern times and reframe it as a series of statements, atheists would have us believe that it is incompatible for the following three conditions to simultaneously exist:

1. God is all-powerful.
2. God is all good.
3. Evil exists.

If God is unable to prevent evil, then He is not all-powerful.

If God is able to prevent evil but is unwilling to do so, then He is evil.

If God is both able and willing to prevent evil, then why does evil still persist?

The atheist's solution? To declare that God doesn't exist.

We'll see in a moment how this "solution" is rife with hypocrisy, inconsistency, and illogic, but first, we need to establish a definition of what evil really is.

The *Cambridge Dictionary* defines evil (adjective) as "morally bad, cruel, or very unpleasant."[2]

The *Oxford English Dictionary* likewise defines evil as "morally depraved, bad, wicked, vicious."[3]

Merriam-Webster defines evil (noun) as "the fact of suffering, misfortune, and wrongdoing."[4]

Are these definitions of evil satisfying? I find brussels sprouts very unpleasant, but does that make them evil? MMA fighter Conor McGregor was vicious in the octagon, but were the rapid movements of his elbows and knees evil? I've had the misfortune of suffering a round of food poisoning thanks to some bad Big Mac sauce, but was it really evil? Clearly, the dictionary definitions of evil rely heavily on moral relativism, which is in no way a sufficient base for a working definition of evil. Nations throughout history have considered all sorts of evils to be good, moral, righteous, and even pleasing to their gods: The Aztecs practiced human sacrifice. The Canaanites practiced polygamy. The Babylonians practiced prostitution *in church*. (The Israelites even built male prostitute shrines in 1 Kings 14:24.) Much of the ancient Middle East practiced incest. The Romans held gladiatorial games. The British hunted witches. Americans enslaved Africans. Germans sent Jews to gas chambers. The Chinese practiced infanticide. Young Muslim men blow up children in cafes. Nearly every rich person on earth reaps interest off the poor. You and I enjoy the benefits of countless cases of deforestation, planetary poisoning, and child labor. Moral relativism is a constant theme in Scripture, from Adam and Eve defining right and wrong on their own terms, to Samson's time when everyone did what was right in their own eyes, to the Tower of Babel, the Golden Calf, the false prophets, and the Pharisees of Matthew 15:1–20, who taught human commands as though they were God's doctrine.

Why is Jesus accused of being demon-possessed, when He is in fact the exact opposite? Because we live in the upside-down world of darkness. Moral relativism is everywhere. When people (including churchgoers) accept the fallen world as it is and presume all is well and right and good, then that which is *truly* well and right and good seems demonic and satanic. Here's just one potent example: The idea of biblical economic reform is an appalling evil to most churchgoers. The Christian economic vision with its laws against interest and certain types of profit, its proportional taxation and allotted land portions for all, its debt jubilees and protections against systemic poverty, are today written off as "communist" and "totalitarian" and surely of the devil's making. When we accept and participate in many aspects of the global economy as it is, we as Christians and churches are, in God's reality, acting satanically.

Jesus predicts moral relativism will get so ugly that He says, "whoever kills [Christians] will think he is offering service to

God." It should be obvious to any student of history that defining evil shouldn't rest on the shifting sands of collective human feeling but on a transcendent and unchanging definition.

Christians define evil quite a bit more clearly than the dictionaries: Evil is disobedience, rebellion, or unfaithfulness to God. Evil is sin and sin is evil. Sin and evil are any intentional or unintentional violations of the word, will, and way of God in thought, word, or deed. Sin in Hebrew is *chata* (to miss). Sin in Greek is *hamartia* (to miss the mark). Sin is to miss God's perfection. Evil is to fall short of the glory of God. Accuser-Adversary is not the source of evil. Rebellion is. The source of evil is missing God.

It is illogical for non-believers to ask why God would allow evil and suffering. You and I do not believe in the existence of flying pink unicorns, so it would be illogical for us to question why flying pink unicorns do *anything*. Atheists and anti-theists forget (or ignore) the fact that "evil" does not and cannot exist without a moral absolute. If the universe is morally neutral, then murder, torture, slavery, and child rape are all just the movement of molecules. Rudeness and verbal cruelty don't exist—that's just Homo sapiens pushing air over vocal cords. Genocide is just the rearrangement of atoms. In an age of growing resource strain, a strong scientific case could be made for culling billions of human beings. Evil is a *spiritual* categorization, not a scientific one. Without God, there is no morality or immorality, no right or wrong, no good or evil. Nothing is better or worse than anything else. Everything is meaningless without God. Economics, politics, marriage, parenthood, art, culture, drama, gastronomy, sport, friendship, love. Without an absolute standard of right and wrong, life is pure chaos. No wonder billions of people live with crippling despair.

The greatest lie in human history—the only one that stretches all the way back to the eve of *adam* in Genesis 3:5—is moral relativism, that we get to decide good from evil. We don't. God alone holds the coherent and comprehensive system of truth and morality, because only God possesses the unified theory science so desperately seeks.

Absolute truth exists, and there's a simple way to perceive its existence with basic logic. Let's say someone declares, "There is no absolute truth." Is that statement absolutely true? If it's false, then absolutes exist. If it's true, then absolutes exist because it is itself a statement of absolute truth. In other words, it is impossible for absolutes *not* to exist. There is either absolute truth or there isn't. Both are absolutes. Therefore absolutes must exist. Existence cannot exist without absolutes. Change is an absolute. Relativity is an absolute. Existence and nonexistence are absolutes. Flux and temporal constructs are, by definition, absolutes.

The lie of moral relativism is extremely dangerous. To deny the existence of an absolute God is to deny real morality—to deny the existence of good and evil. Remember, evil is rebellion against God. If you don't believe in God, then nothing can be truly evil because evil doesn't exist. And if evil doesn't exist, life becomes unacceptably and hopelessly cruel. A stillborn baby is not a profound misfortune, it's just a blip in the scientific process. A teenage suicide is not a tragedy, it's just a slight decrease in the surplus population. A kidnapping of a spouse is just a relocation of mass. A suicide bombing at a funeral is no happier or sadder than a birthday party or a wedding. If anything, in that world-view these are good things, because they show natural selection at work.

Moral relativism inevitably leads to the conflation of shared freedom with individual autonomy. Autonomous people are a law unto themselves. So what happens when eight billion autonomous people have conflicting goals? Chaos. To paraphrase Thucydides, the strong do what they want, and the poor suffer what they must. As Cardinal Joseph Ratzinger (later Pope Benedict XVI) put it, "We are building a dictatorship of relativism that does not recognize anything as definitive and whose ultimate goal consists solely of one's own ego and desires."[6]

The biblical writers didn't envision freedom as autonomy. "To them, freedom was *the ability to do what was right regardless of circumstances.* In other words, modern [Western] 'freedom'—autonomy—is actually a collective anti-freedom."[7]

Let's call this the anti-theodicy problem, or the problem of non-evil.

If there is no God, then there is no absolute moral standard.

If there is no absolute moral standard, then "evil" is decided by the individual.

When two individuals believe opposite things to be evil, the strongest dominates.

Let me be brutally clear: On a long enough time scale, *to deny the existence of God is to consign humanity to slavery.* We've seen this cycle again and again throughout human history. Everyone starts roughly the same, some gain an advantage over others, power compounds generationally until the masses suffer subjugation, at which point there's a violent revolution or world war and the cycle starts all over again.

Can you see how moral relativism is one of the most dangerous things in the universe? Remember, Adolf Hitler didn't think he was evil. When King Charles III's ancestors enslaved and starved and murdered countless Anglo-Saxon families to cement their control of Britain, they believed they were righteous. The Eden lie is that humans are the determiners of right and wrong. It was a poisoned fruit from the very start. (Moral relativism contains a deep irony: If you burn down a relativist's house, they immediately appeal to an objective moral standard. In such a case, you could retort that you were simply trying to stay warm.)

If there is no God, there is no evil. I'll repeat it again because it bears repeating. If there is no God, *there is no evil.* Without a moral absolute, evil does not and cannot exist. It's every man for himself, and only the strongest will survive. Rebellion against God is the definition of evil. Accordingly, the *only* moral position is to believe there is a God whose truths are absolute.

We really must press on atheists' strained rationality here. If God is not real, as they claim, it leads to all sorts of intractable conundrums:

1. If there is no God, then there is no real evil, because evil is a function of moral absolutism. It's illogical to accuse God of being evil—if you don't believe in God, you also don't believe in evil.

2. If there is no God, then it is each human's job to stop that which they individually perceive to be "evil."

3. If there is no God, and two humans perceive two opposite things to be "evil," then who is right and who is wrong? In this scenario, is might right?

4. If there is no God, and any "good" human is aware that any "evil" continues to exist in the world but does not do *everything* in their power to end that "evil," then they are "evil." I have several atheist friends who genuinely believe they are good people, but the continued presence of their fancy houses, boats, cars, appliances, devices, and cottages despite the continued presence of human trafficking and child starvation suggest they are in fact *deeply* malevolent. And we can push this further: If atheists really are the only enlightened ones and yet are not doing everything in their power to right the perceived wrongs around them, then *they above all others* are responsible for the mess we find ourselves in.

How do atheists and anti-theists reconcile this hypocrisy? How can the world simultaneously blame God for the evil in this world, deny His existence, and give themselves a hall pass to allow evil to exist? It's bad-faith argumentation to the core. Even worse, it negates the possibility that love is not only real but is the most powerful force in existence.

Consider the full ramifications of denying God's existence. Not only does evil not exist, but neither does love. Love, after all, is a spiritual construct, as are hope, creativity, justice, forgiveness, gratitude, wisdom, faith, compassion, humility, joy, peace, courage, purpose, intuition, beauty. Without God, none of these things exist. The atheist's love for their child is just chemical reactions and nothing more. The atheist's adoration of their spouse is just oxytocin and dopamine. The atheist's hopes for the future are just serotonin and endorphins. Once again, a denial of God puts us in chains, this time making us slaves to our flesh, our feelings, and our emotions. In this worldview, if the brain chemicals say to do something, we have no choice but to obey. No wonder the world is rife with materialism, egoism, nihilism, addiction, and confusion. These awful conditions are the direct result of God-denialism. (The anti-theist's assault on absolute truth leaves them in a catch-22, too: Without absolute truth, even the statement "everything is meaningless" is therefore meaningless. Like non-absolutes, meaninglessness *cannot* exist, because meaninglessness has a meaning.)

Where does all this God-denialism and moral relativism end? Paul gives his prediction in 2 Timothy 3:1–5.

> But understand this, that in the last days there will come times of difficulty. For people will be lovers of self, lovers of money, proud, arrogant, abusive, disobedient to their parents, ungrateful, unholy, heartless, unappeasable, slanderous, without self-control, brutal, not loving good, treacherous, reckless, swollen with conceit, lovers of pleasure rather than lovers of God, having the appearance of godliness, but denying its power. Avoid such people.

If you need a good indicator of moral relativism, just track how language is used and abused in a given society as definitions start to stray from reality. As Ezra Pound put it, "When words cease to cling close to things, kingdoms fall, empires wane and diminish."[5]

As far as I am concerned, God-deniers have in no way earned the rational right to interrogate Christians about the problem of evil. It takes a repulsive amount of hubris to excoriate Christians for believing in God (even in spite of the theodicy question) compared with the full-on 24/7 loveless, hopeless, graceless, joyless, peaceless, beautyless, purposeless, homicidal, suicidal, irrational alternative that is God-denialism. At the very least, if there's going to be an inquisition, it's only fair to let both sides take the stand to be cross-examined.

Christians, on the other hand, have earned the right to ask the theodicy question. They do not question God's existence. They do not question His goodness. They do not question His omnipotence. And they certainly do not question the existence of evil. Their question is distilled to a single point: *Why* does God allow evil?

Before we can speculate why God allows evil, we need to determine the source of evil. We will not beat around the bush to find it: Evil (rebellion against God) is one of the potential outcomes of giving any being free will.

So, before we can tackle why God allows evil, we need to ask why God gave us free will.

Free Will

It is impossible to make table salt without sodium or chloride. Without those two base elements, table salt wouldn't exist and no one would eat at McDonald's.

Free will is a base element of love. Free will is a nonnegotiable prerequisite for the possibility of love to exist. Imagine my wife was a robot or a slave, and every time I pressed her, she said, "I love you." Is that real love or compelled lip service? Love can only exist when a free will chooses love over rejection. God *had* to give us free will so we could choose to love Him. Anything less would make Him not good.

Before we can talk about free will, we need to talk about what free will is not. Free will is not ultimate human self-determination. Free will is not self-sovereignty. Hardcore libertarians believe human choices spring up spontaneously and not from any prior causes. The libertarian notion of free will is pure delusion because everything except God himself has a prior cause. It's silly to believe our choices have zero prior causes—we are affected by everything from our genes and upbringing and parents and politics to moon cycles and how many hours our baby cried through the night, never mind major macro influences like the laws of nature, our sin nature, Accuser-Adversary's testing, and God's ultimate plan. Human free will is only free up to the point that it has the ability to act according to its own nature, which itself is influenced and corrupted by billions of other free wills.

The first act of free will is to believe in free will. The second act of free will is to accept that even free will has its limits. Clearly, free will is limited: I would like to fly, but gravity has other plans. I would like to live to be one thousand years old, but being a sedentary writer all but guarantees a much shorter lifespan (and neck problems for the duration).

Our free will is also hindered by the choices of other free wills, as stated. North Koreans have free will, but Kim Jong Un's free will is stronger. The dictatorship's decision to lock its people in a giant slave colony and control their access to knowledge has serious implications for their ability to freely choose. Even Kim Jong Un is subject to stronger free wills—namely, the presidents of China and Russia who support a North Korean puppet regime to create a buffer between themselves and American-allied South Korea. Tens of millions suffer a serious lack of free will because of these tensions, including the Kim family.

My two-year-old son, Concord, has free will, but my free will is stronger. My free will has already taught him the alphabet and how to cut broccoli stems and sort the trash from recycling, and it has kept him from getting run over by multiple cars.

When two free wills collide, whose should take priority? That which is stronger? Smarter? Wiser? Or that which is all-knowing, all-present, all-powerful, and all-loving?

Let's never forget that God has a free will of His own. The utter idiocy of our rebellion against God proves how truly undeserving of free will we are. We aren't playing fair. Why doesn't our loving God get to have a free will? Would we deny Him that and in doing so prove ourselves evil beyond our own understanding? It wouldn't be loving of God to not let us exercise our free will and it's equally unloving for us to not want God to exercise His free will. Human will is at work in the world, and God's will is at work in the world. We cannot override His will, He does not override our free will, and He wishes to partner with human wills to achieve His will. This is a profound mystery.

Free-willed spirits are at work all around us. I am a spirit, you are a spirit, Accuser-Adversary is a spirit, God is a spirit. As far as we can tell, all spirits have free wills. Free wills can plant thought seeds in our minds, and we can choose to water them, fertilize them, or drown them. In the Bible, God saves King Abimelech's life by appearing to him in a dream and warning him not to sleep with Abraham's wife, Sarah (Genesis 20). God performs multiple signs to convince a stuttering Egyptian ex-aristocrat named Moses to lead His people out of slavery (Exodus 4). God reveals to the prophet Samuel the hidden whereabouts of the future king Saul in 1 Samuel 10. God blinds Saul of Tarsus on the road to Damascus in Acts 9. God hardens Pharaoh's heart in Exodus 9:12 but then softens the heart of Lydia in Acts 16:14.

Notice that God never physically forces humans to do His will. Not once in all of Scripture does He override a human will. He definitely influences or intervenes in human affairs in various ways: He plants thoughts and dreams, gives signs and wonders, appears in various shapes and forms, maims and even kills—but He never violates a human will. God can kill us, but He doesn't make us kill. God can send His rebellious people into slavery in

Egypt or Babylon, but He won't force anyone to enslave others. He always leaves the choice up to the human to decide whether to obey or rebel.

In addition to intervening by His own will, God also regularly intervenes due to the will of human beings. God frees the enslaved Israelites from Egypt because of their prayerful groans (Exodus 2:23–25). God roasts Sodom and Gomorrah because an outcry went up against them (Genesis 18:20). God breaks Peter out of King Herod's jail in Acts 12 because of a prayer meeting. God allows the Israelites to expressly go against His perfect will and anoint a human king (1 Samuel 8:4–22). God adds fifteen years to King Hezekiah's life because of his supplications (2 Kings 20:1–11). God relents from destroying Nineveh after Jonah's halfhearted preaching led the city-state to fast and pray (Jonah 3:1–10).

Human free will can and absolutely does sway God's will. Just look at Jeremiah 18:7–10. "If at any time I declare concerning a nation or a kingdom, that I will pluck up and break down and destroy it, and if that nation, concerning which I have spoken, turns from its evil, I will relent of the disaster that I intended to do to it. And if at any time I declare concerning a nation or a kingdom that I will build and plant it, and if it does evil in my sight, not listening to my voice, then I will relent of the good that I had intended to do to it."

Intervention often requires intercession. Clearly, human free wills can overpower other human free wills. Any warlord, dictator, or tyrant can impose his will on the masses. But God loves to act in concert with human wills. Christians can offer up their free will to God's will and allow Him to work in and through their free will to fulfill His ultimate purposes. God can intervene in human free will when a human free will invites Him to do so. When we pray "your kingdom come, your will be done," we give God permission to work His will and establish His sovereign kingdom over humankind.

Discernment is so important here. It's easy to delude ourselves into thinking something is God's will when it's actually just our will. Any prayer we pray that's outside the ultimate will of God will be answered with a hard no. That's why so many Christians experience powerless prayer lives—they're asking for thousands of things that are outside of God's will. So what's the point of praying? This is huge: By constantly communing with Christ, we can align our will with God's and begin to willfully pray the prayers *that unlock His power to act* in human affairs. Put another way: God has a will. Humans have a will. God wants Christians to align with His will and ask His will to be done so He can act.

Where there's a will, there's a way. Unfortunately, every human will is headed the wrong way. Only God's way is the right way. It's telling that before Christianity was called Christianity, it was called the Way.

Accuser-Adversary cannot force a human to sin. If I offer you a bowl of cooked white rice, you can say yes, no, or choose something healthier like Häagen-Dazs vanilla ice cream. (Seriously, look it up.) My offer does not violate your free will. I can test and tempt you with all sorts of other unhealthy foods, but only you can make yourself unhealthy by saying yes. Accuser-Adversary cannot cram sin down our throats like we are foie gras geese, and neither will God force-feed us righteousness and salvation.

Quick recap: The human will is free to follow its own nature, but beyond that it is limited by space and time, by science, the free will of God, Accuser-Adversary, and other spirits past and present, including human free wills. The human free will can also impress itself upon other free wills, including God's. If we want to get hyper-biblical, the human will isn't actually free at all—it's chained in bondage to sin (John 8:34; Romans 6:16; Romans 7:14; 2 Timothy 2:26; 2 Peter 2:19). The human will isn't so much a free will as an enslaved will. We can resist all external compulsion and act according to our nature, but that nature is still a sin nature. Paradoxically, the only thing that can free our enslaved will is to willingly become a slave to the only being with unlimited free will, God himself (1 Corinthians 7:22; Romans 6:18). By allowing the

Holy Spirit to adopt the Father's will in our lives, we become as truly free as any human being can ever possibly be.

And so the drama escalates: Which path would free-willed humans choose—the loving faithfulness that God desires or the active rebellion that creates evil?

Predestination

The moment Adam and Eve chose rebellion over relationship, God didn't freak out, slamming the big red emergency button on His control-room dashboard, with heaven's alarm system blaring the warning: "Alert, alert, unforeseen sin on planet Earth. All hands on deck. Scramble the angels. Back to the *logos* drawing board. All seraphim to the boardroom for an emergency strategy session on how to combat this blindside surprise."

No.

Humanity's rebellion was no more of an ambush for God than Accuser-Adversary's rebellion was. The all-knowing, all-powerful, all-present, eternal Trinity was not caught off guard, bushwhacked, dumbfounded, or bamboozled. Christ wasn't flabbergasted. The Holy Spirit didn't lose His breath. God the Father wasn't flummoxed with perplexity. They'd had it in hand since before creation.

When my wife and I decided we'd try to get pregnant, we had no idea God would bless us with a beautiful little boy named Concord. But from the moment we found out Michelle was pregnant, we had a pretty good idea that our future son wouldn't be perfect. We chose to have Concord despite knowing he would disappoint us, dismay us, disobey us, and even hurt others. God did the same thing in creating beings with free will, except He knew *exactly* how we'd rebel against His perfect plan.

God was prepared for Accuser-Adversary's rebellion, and He was ready with a plan for humankind's rebellion too. The first step was to rescue Adam and Eve from living forever. It's a strange thought, but think about it for a second. If God hadn't driven humanity's first couple out of the garden of Eden—if He'd allowed them to eat of the tree of life—humans would have lived forever in sin, in darkness, and in eternal separation from God. A living hell, forever. Physical death was God's loving way of ensuring humans the possibility of eternal life in heaven without being cut off from Him.

This should give us something of an idea about how serious God is about love. God willingly created humanity with free will, despite knowing we would choose rebellion and plunge the world into chaos, debt, for-profit landlording, war, rape, murder, torture, slavery, species collapse, and the brink of nuclear annihilation. That's how committed God is to love. That's how committed God is to you. To be sure, He is still the God of justice who doesn't let sin go unpunished—that's precisely why Jesus had to come to earth—but His overarching goal is to fill the universe with His love, and He was willing to run the risk of our sinning to achieve that.

But it's all a bit hard to wrap our minds around, isn't it? The best way I've found to describe God's sovereignty to the teens in my Sunday school class is this: Picture the universe. Now picture an unlimited multiverse with every possible combination and permutation of events. If you turn left, that's one universe. If your friend turns right, that's a different universe. If you stand, sit, jump, sneeze, kill, or make a horrible decision like eating an all-spinach salad, whatever you do, it's a different universe. God, being so epically all-powerful and all-everywhere, has already seen every possible universe of actions. And here's the exciting part: Even though He probably has one ultimate perfect path, He has *also* designed a life invitation for each of us in every single possible universe. I don't know if that's helpful for you, but teens have good imaginations and seem to grasp it. God is everywhere, including the everywheres that He didn't want to exist, and the perfect everywheres that will never exist because of our rebellion. In other words, God foresaw Accuser-Adversary's rebellion, your rebellion, and my rebellion, and created a roadmap to heaven that accounted for sin, death, suffering, slavery, all of it. God allows bad things to happen but has a plan for each outcome—an invitation to abide in His presence.

So does this mean humans are predestined for heaven or hell? It depends on who you ask. On one end, you've got the hardcore John Calvin predestinationists who say God picked His favorites (the elect) before the beginning of time and damned everyone else (the reprobate) for eternity, and on the other end, you've got the hardcore Jacobus Arminius Arminians who believe it's all up to us. I don't like false dichotomies. God's will is that *every single person* commits to a relationship with Him (1 Timothy 2:3–4; 2 Peter 3:9; John 3:16–17; Acts 17:30–31; Romans 10:12–13; Revelation 22:17), but He also gives us free will to reject Him so that love can have the opportunity to exist. A one-way relationship is not a relationship. Perhaps there is a perfect universe in which all human beings, predestined to spend eternity with God, choose to love Him wholeheartedly. But billions of free wills not choosing rebellion was always a long shot. The collective human destiny was supposed to be unity with its Creator, but destinies are daily thwarted by the decisions we make.

This middle position between Calvinism and Arminianism is called Molinism, named after a sixteenth-century Spanish Jesuit named Luis de Molina. Molinists believe God has "middle knowledge" of all possible events, scenarios, and outcomes, and can use them to fulfill His purposes without violating human free will. If God knows I will do X when I encounter Y, He can actualize a world where I encounter Y so I freely choose X so He can accomplish purpose Z. Human free will, meet God's foreknowledge.

That's not to say it still isn't God who gets the complete and total glory for every single salvation. Our natural, fallen, sin-laden, fleshy free will would and could never willingly choose to love God (1 Corinthians 2:14; Romans 3:11 and 8:7; 9:16; John 1:13). It was God who offered the proposal, wooed us to accept it (John 6:44), and gave us the ability to accept it (Deuteronomy 29:4; 30:6; Ezekiel 36:26; John 6:37, 63, 65; Ephesians 1:4–6; 2 Timothy 1:9).

God never forces love, but He occasionally ossifies self-hardened hearts (Exodus 9:12; John 12:40; Romans 9:18). The worst fate imaginable is for God to give us our disordered desires.

The truth of His nature goes out to all people (Romans 1:20), but God already knows the final score. Check out Revelation 13:8 in the NIV—"All inhabitants of the earth will worship the beast—all whose names have not been written in the Lamb's book of life, the Lamb who was slain from the creation of the world." Before God created the universe, before He created the heavens and the earth, before He created Adam and Eve and the fruit in Eden, God already knew the names of those who, empowered by His spirit, would say yes to His marriage proposal (Acts 13:48; Romans 8:29–30). He knew every single person who would receive His salvation based on His wooing. Their names are in the book of life. Human free will, meet God's free will.

But what about all the evil in this world that isn't caused by free will?

Natural Evil

Let's say for a moment that we can bring ourselves to complete the extremely difficult task of trusting God will eventually right every wrong and punish every biblically defined evil committed by murderers, rapists, kidnappers, terrorists, politicians, bankers, shareholders, and the like. But what about "natural" evils like floods and hurricanes and forest fires? Sure, human evil requires consciousness and intent, so mudslides and volcanoes are not evil in the classical human sense, but even when you factor out all the unright-way-of-livingness of human choices like shoddy dam construction and building on floodplains and irresponsible forest stewardship, who is to be held responsible for what remains?

The answer, whether we like it or not, is *we are*. The physical world is subject to the curse of sin. As hard as it is to swallow, the truth is that even a child dying of cancer is the result of the collective fall caused by humanity's free-will rebellion. As God said to Adam in Genesis 3:17, "cursed is the ground because of you." Remember, the world is not as it was or will be. God allowed human free will despite knowing we could and would unlock the door to fallenness and sin and death, because He wanted to open the door of love. Until He completes His redemption plan, the earth lies under future judgment because of sin: "The earth lies defiled under its inhabitants; for they have transgressed the laws, violated the statutes, broken the everlasting covenant. Therefore a curse devours the earth, and its inhabitants suffer for their guilt; therefore the inhabitants of the earth are scorched. . . . The earth is utterly broken, the earth is split apart, the earth is violently shaken. The earth staggers like a drunken man" (Isaiah 24:5–6, 19–20).

But God is a God of justice. He is a righteous judge who feels indignation every single day (Psalm 7:11). He is storing up wrath (Romans 9:22). A day of wrath is coming (Revelation 6:16–17). His wrath will fall on the rebellious (Ephesians 5:6). He promises to avenge (Nahum 1:2). We can firmly believe God will set all things right. No evil deed will go unpunished—not Accuser-Adversary's, not the atheist's, not the Christian's. The only difference for Jesus-followers is that the iniquity, liability, and punishment for our sins has been dropped on Jesus (Isaiah 53:6; 2 Corinthians 5:21). But even the immense weight of sin didn't crush Him to death—He died by choice when He knew all was fulfilled, then rose again in triumph. It requires great faith to trust that God's decision to give us free will despite all the evil we have caused is ultimately the right decision.

So what are we to do with all the suffering in the meantime? Console ourselves with a vague notion of celestial comeuppance and restitution once we're all long gone? Paul adopts the right mindset in Romans 8:18–23.

> For I consider that the sufferings of this present time are not worth comparing with the glory that is to be revealed to us. For

the creation waits with eager longing for the revealing of the sons of God. For the creation was subjected to futility, not willingly, but because of him who subjected it, in hope that the creation itself will be set free from its bondage to corruption and obtain the freedom of the glory of the children of God. For we know that the whole creation has been groaning together in the pains of childbirth until now. And not only the creation, but we ourselves, who have the firstfruits of the Spirit, groan inwardly as we wait eagerly for adoption as sons, the redemption of our bodies.

This is a brutal passage to contemplate. Paul and his friends suffered immensely—including the torture and murder of their families, friends, and selves—and *he doesn't even consider those sufferings worthy of comparison to the coming revelation.* Again we find ourselves compelled to right-size God and right-size suffering. The loss of a child or spouse is undeniably horrific, but if we could experience heaven for even a moment, our pain would be so blunted we would burst into jubilant worship at every Christian funeral. As much as we yearn to have our loved ones back with us, it would be a great evil to snatch the departed out of God's manifest presence and drag them back to this rotting world of sin.

Love required free will. Free will chose sin. Sin led to universal fallenness, suffering, and death. Love promises to conquer sin, suffering, and death in such a way that transforms free will to exclusively choose love for eternity. Writers are encouraged to refrain from using exclamation marks, but *how great is our God*?! His love conquers all.

And yet we still groan for redemption. You can feel David's loins-deep yearning for redemption in Psalm 10, and it's a master class in how to pray in anguish, hope, and righteous zeal:

> Why, O LORD, do you stand far away?
> Why do you hide yourself in times of trouble?

In arrogance the wicked hotly pursue the poor;
>   let them be caught in the schemes that they have
>   devised.
For the wicked boasts of the desires of his soul,
>   and the one greedy for gain curses and renounces the
>   LORD.
In the pride of his face the wicked does not seek him;
>   all his thoughts are, "There is no God."
His ways prosper at all times;
>   your judgments are on high, out of his sight;
>   as for all his foes, he puffs at them.
He says in his heart, "I shall not be moved;
>   throughout all generations I shall not meet adversity."
His mouth is filled with cursing and deceit and
>   oppression;
>   under his tongue are mischief and iniquity.
He sits in ambush in the villages;
>   in hiding places he murders the innocent.
His eyes stealthily watch for the helpless;
>   he lurks in ambush like a lion in his thicket;
he lurks that he may seize the poor;
>   he seizes the poor when he draws him into his net.
The helpless are crushed, sink down,
>   and fall by his might.
He says in his heart, "God has forgotten,
>   he has hidden his face, he will never see it."
Arise, O LORD; O God, lift up your hand;
>   forget not the afflicted.
Why does the wicked renounce God
>   and say in his heart, "You will not call to account"?
But you do see, for you note mischief and vexation,
>   that you may take it into your hands;
to you the helpless commits himself;
>   you have been the helper of the fatherless.
Break the arm of the wicked and evildoer;
>   call his wickedness to account till you find none.

The LORD is king forever and ever;
　　the nations perish from his land.
O LORD, you hear the desire of the afflicted;
　　you will strengthen their heart; you will incline your
　　　ear
to do justice to the fatherless and the oppressed,
　　so that man who is of the earth may strike terror no
　　　more.

One of our great acts of faith is to believe that Christ is preeminent above all created beings and that God is keeping score. Justice will be served in its entirety. But sometimes the pain and loss are too much for a human soul to bear, aren't they? God made a plan for that, too. When we're so low that we can't even muster the words to pray, Romans 8:26 says "the Spirit himself intercedes for us with groanings too deep for words."

So what are we to do in times of extreme suffering? We are to trust God to such an extent that we don't even bother an attempt at understanding His coming reconciliation. We are to groan for redemption and let God's spirit groan alongside us, moment by heartrending moment, until that glorious day when "He will wipe away every tear from their eyes, and death shall be no more, neither shall there be mourning, nor crying, nor pain anymore, for the former things have passed away" (Revelation 21:4).

This is what it means to live by faith. It is this unshakable faith in Jesus that accrues to our account as righteousness before a holy God. Is anything worth more than faith in Christ? Can anything sustain the human soul through its darkest nights more than the radiant love of our Father?

Setting Everything Right

Here's what we know for sure: In the God-denying construct, the world is still evil but we can no longer call it evil, and as the world increasingly rebels against God, the world becomes significantly more evil while calling it good. In the God-affirming reality, Christians can practice faith and trust in the hope that the God of justice will be true to His Word. When we face the endless evils caused by free-will rebellion against God's will, there are four bedrock truths about God we must embrace:

1. *He will work it out.*

God is working *everything*, absolutely everything, toward His ultimate purpose. We won't see God's full move-by-move game plan until we reach the conclusion, but when we do, we will be dumbfounded by His brilliance. Our greatest act of faith is holding fast to the belief that God is sovereign. God has a plan to make right and redeem every murder, rape, drowning, enslavement, torture, OxyContin addiction, and mortgage foreclosure. We must muster the confidence of Romans 8:28 to declare, "We know that for those who love God all things work together for good, for those who are called according to his purpose."

2. *He will wipe away every tear.*

Again, Revelation 21:4 (plus v. 5), "He will wipe away every tear from their eyes, and death shall be no more, neither shall there be mourning, nor crying, nor pain anymore, for the former things have passed away. And he who was seated on the throne said, 'Behold, I am making all things new.'"

The old life of pain and sin and suffering and evil? It's dead. It passed away. All things? Brand spanking new.

3. *He will blot out the memory.*

In Isaiah 65:17, God promises, "I create new heavens and a new earth, and the former things shall not be remembered or come into mind." Imagine you lived one of the worst possible lives ever lived on planet Earth—a tortured child sex slave locked for life in a basement dungeon in an Indian brothel. Remember, this was not God's plan or God's doing. Hideously evil and satanic men chose rebellion against God and violence against your person, and for reasons we can never possibly fathom aside from needing to keep the option of love open, God allowed their free-will actions to continue. But unlike in the God-denier's world, there is good news for the faithful: The very millisecond you die, you instantly wake up and live for eternity in the radiant, glorious presence of God, and *not once for all time will you even for a nanosecond* remember your hellish life on earth. No memories. No nightmares. No lingering anxiety. No body keeping score. No post-traumatic stress disorder. The good, the bad, the ugly, the demonic, and the satanic are all gone, forever. Hallelujah.

4. *He will deliver pleasure that pales the pain.*

The apostle Paul is the textbook example of a Christian who experienced huge amounts of suffering at the hands of an evil and fallen creation. He experienced "weaknesses, insults, hardships, persecutions, and calamities" (2 Corinthians 12:10). He was whipped thirty-nine times on five different occasions, beaten three times with rods, was nearly stoned to death, experienced three shipwrecks, and was constantly in danger, experiencing sleeplessness, hunger, thirst, and cold exposure (2 Corinthians 11:24–28). Paul knew he was a dead man walking (2 Timothy 4:6–8) and his earthly life ended when he was brutally beheaded by Nero around 67 AD. Yet what does Paul say in 2 Corinthians 4:17? "For this *light momentary affliction* is preparing for us an eternal weight of glory beyond all comparison" (emphasis added).

It's extremely cold comfort, but unlike the unbelieving world, Christians can at least take comfort in the fact that all suffering is comparatively light and momentary, and that the eternal weight of glory will press the previous pain into nonexistence. It's impossible to fathom without the Holy Spirit, but even the worst pain, suffering, and torture on earth is *not even worth comparing* with the glory to come (Romans 8:18).

Why God Allows Evil

We finally return to the question that started this chapter. Christians have earned the right to ask the theodicy question because they do not question God's existence, His goodness, His omnipotence, or the existence of evil. Our question is sharpened to a single point: Why does God allow evil?

Let's use the same framework atheists use to pose the theodicy question.

A. If God is all powerful, can He not prevent evil from existing?

Yes, He can prevent evil from existing, but compelled good is not good. Choosing not to prevent evil is not the same thing as being unable to prevent evil. God remains all-powerful.

B. If God is all good, should He not prevent evil from existing?

No. He would not be all good if He prevented free will. God gave us free will because He is good, and we chose rebellion and created evil. God remains all good.

C. If evil exists, then either God is not all-powerful or not all good.

False. Evil exists because God is all-powerful and all good, and gave us the free will to obey or reject Him. The real problem of evil is that humans have not only sinned by falling short of God's absolute perfection, but also that we have the gall to simultaneously pretend sin doesn't exist and define good and evil on our own terms.

Stated another way:

1. God is all-powerful.
2. God is all good.
3. God in love gave humanity the free will to choose good or evil.
4. Evil exists because humanity chose evil. Free-will rebellion is the cause of all evil in the universe, including natural evil.
5. God knew free wills would choose evil, so He created a plan to conquer evil with love.
6. God continues to allow free will to exist because His plan is not finished.
7. Our mission is to trust, hope, obey, and remain faithful until we meet Him face-to-face.
8. God will enact justice, make all things right, wipe away every tear, blot out every memory, and deliver pleasure beyond all pain.

But here's the thing. John 1:3 says, "All things were made through him, and without him was not any thing made that was made." Revelation 4:11 says, "Worthy are you, our Lord and God, to receive glory and honor and power, for you created all things, and by your will they existed and were created." Does that mean God created evil? Did God create murder and rape and interest and genocide? Saint Augustine had the epiphany that evil is *not a thing*. It's a perversion, an abstraction. It doesn't have an actual being, spirit, matter, or substance. The best way we can understand this is in terms of light and darkness. Light exists in real scientific terms, in waves and particles. Darkness, however, is just a lack of light. Genesis 1:31 says everything God created was "very good." Good and evil aren't opposites—evil is just the lack of God's goodness. Evil is a falling short. Evil is a lack of light. First John 1:5 says God is pure light and zero darkness.

This is a bit of a mind-bender, but even though God didn't create evil, everything was created for God. Even Accuser-Adversary. Even evil. Colossians 1:15–16 says that Jesus "is the image of the invisible God, the firstborn of all creation. For by him all things were created, in heaven and on earth, visible and invisible, whether thrones or dominions or rulers or authorities—all things were created through him and for him."

> Heaven and earth? Through Him and for Him.
> Angels and demons? Through Him and for Him.
> Panthers, ravens, black-backed gulls? Through Him and for Him.
> Communism and capitalism? Through Him and for Him.
> Dictators, tyrants, and some mothers-in-law? Through Him and for Him.
> Accuser-Adversary? Through Him and for Him.
> Murder? Through Him and for Him.
> Slavery? Through Him and for Him.
> Good and evil? Through Him and for Him.

Note that evil was created through God and for God, but not *by* God. If you had created oxygen and hydrogen, that doesn't make you the inventor of water. God created the atomic elements with a vast number of wonderful, yet-to-be-discovered purposes, but He didn't create the atomic bomb. God created oxygen, hydrogen, nitrogen, palladium, carbon, and corn, but it was humans who created the fentanyl that is killing hundreds of image-bearers every single day.

Remember, evil is rebellion against God. For people who don't believe in the existence of God, nothing is truly evil because no absolute definition of evil exists. In the Christian framework, evil is defined as rebellion against God. Evil = God's perfection minus free-will deviation. So the question "Why does God allow evil?" is the same as asking "Why does God allow rebellion?" God created free will in hopes that we would love Him, but we create evil every time we choose rebellion. God did not create evil any more than He created canoes, zip-lining, or spaghetti Bolognese. God gave us everything we needed to create a flourishing life in relationship with Him, and we chose rebellion in every area of life. In the same way God had to open the door to the possibility of race-targeting nanoweapons when He created the elements that allow us to breathe and grow food, He had to create the possibility of evil in order to give us the free will to choose love. Love is His ultimate purpose, and it is clearly worth far more to Him than we can accept or imagine.

So if evil was created through and for Him but not by Him, what is God using evil to achieve?

Here it is: Without evil, humanity could never know the fullness of God. If created beings like us and Accuser-Adversary didn't create evil, we would never experience His grace. We would never know His justice. We would never see the height and width and depth of His love. Without evil, there would be no need for Jesus to show us the apotheosis of love by sacrificing himself for His enemies. Evil was created through and for God so He could reveal His fullness so we could experience transformational awe at the wonder of His greatness. God allowed free-willed spirits to create evil so He could show us the depths of His love. God allows evil to continue because He wants to keep free will and the possibility of love on the table, all while ensuring that evil helps accomplish His goal of redemption.

Why does God allow evil? Asking this question inevitably leads us to one massively huge, stunningly beautiful, terrifyingly grand conclusion: *Evil exists because God's love is the most important thing in the universe.*

That's not to say God's love requires evil to exist, of course. His love existed for eons before sin and will do so well after sin has been destroyed for all time. But Christians must choose to accept this truth in the bottom of their souls: God has seen fit that it is better to have free will and the possibility of both love and rebellion than it is to have no free will and no love. A world without free will and love is pure evil. *Love was the only way.* The story of God is the story of love coming full circle: Love created free will. Free will created rebellion/evil. Rebellion/evil created death. Jesus saw it all beforehand and chose to die to create everlasting life. If you hate evil, then the only rational response is wholehearted submission to God's loving will in all things. The life of faith is an invitation into total trust that all of life's sin and pain and suffering and heartbreak and death will not only be made right, but that these things are in our eternal best interest.

In our next chapter, we'll discover how Christians can use these incredible truths to make Accuser-Adversary work for us and our King.

10

THE SERVANT SERPENT

How to Use the Devil to Serve God

"The Devil, if thou wouldest understand it, is even profitable to us,
if we use him aright, and benefits us greatly."

—John Chrysostom, *Against Those Who Object Because
the Devil Has Not Been Put Out of the World*

THERE MAY NEVER BE a better judoka than Yasuhiro Yamashita.
The Japanese judo master holds the record for the longest unbroken victory streak in the sport's history, running to 203 straight wins. In 1984, he won the Olympic gold medal *with a broken toe and a torn calf muscle.* The key to judo, I'm told, is balance and leverage, and the trick is to use your opponent's strength and momentum against them. It's the same in the spiritual realm. The harder Accuser-Adversary comes at you, the harder you can slam

him to the ground. The greater the sin and evil, the greater the opportunity for God's glory and victory.

One could summarize Martin Luther's *The Bondage of the Will* in one sentence: The devil is God's devil. God uses Accuser-Adversary to serve His ultimate purpose, and Christians can use him in the same manner. Before we discuss how to use Accuser-Adversary to our personal benefit and heavenly profitability, we need to ask the major question: What is God's ultimate purpose for humanity? Scripture comes at the question from several angles:

> Ephesians 1:7–10: "In [Jesus] we have redemption through his blood, the forgiveness of our trespasses, according to the riches of his grace, which he lavished upon us, in all wisdom and insight making known to us the mystery of his will, according to his purpose, which he set forth in Christ as a plan for the fullness of time, to unite all things in him, things in heaven and things on earth."
>
> Colossians 1:19–20: "For in him all the fullness of God was pleased to dwell, and through him to reconcile to himself all things, whether on earth or in heaven, making peace by the blood of his cross."
>
> Second Corinthians 5:18–19: "All this is from God, who through Christ reconciled us to himself and gave us the ministry of reconciliation; that is, in Christ God was reconciling the world to himself, not counting their trespasses against them, and entrusting to us the message of reconciliation."

Paul certainly seems to think God's ultimate purpose is to redeem and reconcile all things to himself through Jesus. Romans 8:28 says God is working all things together for the good of those who love Him and are called according to His purpose. Romans

11:36 says, "For [out of] him and through him and to him are all things." When Paul says all things, he really means *all* things, including evil, and real things like Accuser-Adversary.

It's hard for us as humans to wrap our minds around this. If you're reading this as a parent, would you go back and refuse to conceive your son or daughter if you knew 100 percent they'd grow up to be a serial killer? Or would you still roll the dice and hope that your loving parenting could change the outcome? God saw every possible version of how things could play out, including the version where Accuser-Adversary remained a righteous, anointed, loving servant of the holy God. But out of love, God gave him free will, and Accuser-Adversary let the Father down.

The question, of course, is why didn't God just stop Accuser-Adversary as soon as he started? God could have imprisoned him, banished him, evaporated him. He could have parked him on the sun or the dark side of Jupiter's smallest moon. And I think the answer is obvious: Because if it wasn't the devil who rebelled first, it would have been you or me. Giving all beings free will and then stamping out those who rebel is like playing a game of Whac-A-Mole. Not only would the game never end, but it would more or less defeat the entire construct of free will. Accuser-Adversary was the first to fall into sin, but he certainly wouldn't be the last. So, instead of incinerating or incarcerating Accuser-Adversary, God decided to use this first of many sinners to lead many more to righteousness. God's plan is to redeem and reconcile all things, and He temporarily allows evil and Accuser-Adversary to exist because it's part of His redemption and reconciliation plan.

Like the greatest judo master in history, God uses Accuser-Adversary in at least seven ways to bring about His ultimate aim.[1]

1. *God uses Accuser-Adversary to repulse sinners.*

    Evil is often tempting and seductive, but sometimes it's so overmuch that evil becomes repulsive. Like the prodigal son who came to his senses while coveting feed from a pig trough, I have a friend who came to a conviction of sin when he woke up drunk and bleeding in a ditch. I've heard countless testimonies of people whose sin eventually got so bad that it repulsed them in the direction of heaven. The more pain Accuser-Adversary inflicts on the world, the more people are driven toward Christ. The First Great Awakening happened in the tense lead-up to the American Revolution. The American Civil War sparked a revival in both north and south. (D. L. Moody became a famous preacher among the Union troops, and God used the slave-owning Confederate James P. Boyce to found the Southern Baptist Theological Seminary, which later defied Kentucky state law and desegregated its campus.) Nearly all the great hymns of the Christian faith were penned during times of trouble and tumult, including the Reformation, the Industrial Revolution, and the American and French Revolutions. Church attendance soared during the post-World War II awakening.

2. *God uses Accuser-Adversary to harden rebellionists.*

God allows Accuser-Adversary to pluck the gospel out of some people's minds. In the parable of the seeds and soil in Mark 4:15, Jesus says, "When they hear, Satan immediately comes and takes away the word that is sown in them." Second Corinthians 4:4 says, "The god of this world has blinded the minds of the unbelievers, to keep them from seeing the light of the gospel of the glory of Christ." Or, take the example of the Egyptian Pharaoh who enslaved millions of Israelites. The Pharaoh hardens his heart again and again, and eventually, God ossifies it to stone and sinks him to the bottom of the Red Sea (Exodus 15:4). God is long-suffering and merciful, but sometimes, He lets people have what they want. Occasionally, God even lets Accuser-Adversary play his hand so far that it wipes out a huge swath of evil people (like the Nazis) while driving millions of people, soft-hearted, back toward Christ. In the most extreme judo move of all time, God allowed Accuser-Adversary to partner with Judas in betraying Jesus to the Jewish and Roman elites, which opened the door to the salvation of the entire human race.

3. *God uses Accuser-Adversary to strengthen Christians.*

Check out Job 42:11 (emphasis added): "Then all his brothers, sisters, and former friends came and feasted with him in his home. And they consoled him and comforted him because of all the trials *the* LORD had brought against him." It was God working through Accuser-Adversary to strengthen Job's faith. Jesus does the same thing with Peter and the disciples in Luke 22:31–32. "Simon, Simon, behold, Satan demanded to have you [plural], that he might sift you [plural] like wheat, but I have prayed for you [singular] that your [singular] faith may not fail. And when you [singular] have turned again, strengthen your [singular] brothers." Remarkable, right? God allows Accuser-Adversary to test Peter, knowing full well he'll deny his Lord and Savior, but once righteous regret had beaten Peter's rebellion out of him like hammer blows on an anvil to forge a sword, Peter would be strong enough to strengthen thousands of others.

This is not the only time Jesus explicitly points out Accuser-Adversary's relationship with His lead disciple.

From that time Jesus began to show his disciples that he must go to Jerusalem and suffer many things from the elders and chief priests and scribes, and be killed, and on the third day be raised. And Peter took him aside and began to rebuke him, saying, "Far be it from you, Lord! This shall never happen to you." But he turned and said to Peter, "Get behind me, Satan! You are a hindrance to me. For you are not setting your mind on the things of God, but on the things of man."

Matthew 16:21–23

Ironically, if Peter had managed to convince Jesus to cancel Easter, Peter would have damned himself, the rest of the disciples, and you and me forever. God allowed Accuser-Adversary to test Peter to see if he was all wheat or if some weeds still remained. Peter's three denials of Jesus took a brutal toll on his emotions, but that sifting by Accuser-Adversary cemented Simon the fisherman as Peter the apostle.

Every battle, setback, sin, evil, and suffering we face is an opportunity to reject the satanic and grow our faith in God's ultimate sovereignty. None of us will ever come close to perfect on this practice, but imagine if we could meet every trial we faced with a heart and mind fixed in faith on His sovereignty: *God has allowed this. It is now part of His plan for the redemption and reconciliation of all things. My job is to pass the test by staying faithful.*

4. *God uses Accuser-Adversary to discipline disobedient disciples.*

There's an absolutely wild passage in 1 Kings 22:19–23 that rarely is preached in church. The prophet Micaiah says to the kings of Israel and Judah,

> I saw the LORD sitting on his throne, and all the host of heaven standing beside him on his right hand and on his left; and the LORD said, "Who will entice Ahab, that he may go up and fall at Ramoth-gilead?" And one said one thing, and another said another. Then a spirit came forward and stood before the LORD, saying, "I will entice him." And the LORD said to him, "By what means?" And he said, "I will go out, and will be a lying spirit in the mouth of all his prophets." And he said, "You are to entice him, and you shall succeed; go out and do so." Now therefore behold, the LORD has put a lying spirit in the mouth of all these your prophets; the LORD has declared disaster for you.

How crazy is that? Fallen spirits lie constantly, but God's greater purpose always prevails. Sometimes, that even means they get to lie through prophets in order to bait disobedient kings like Ahab. God does something similar with Saul when he starts to stray, sending him a spirit of distress that torments him (1 Samuel 16:14).

The apostle Paul clearly saw Accuser-Adversary's disciplining feature as useful to Christians and the church. In his first letter to the church in Corinth, he calls them out for allowing a churchgoer to commit incest with his father's wife. The solution? "When you are assembled in the name of the Lord Jesus and my spirit is present, with the power of our Lord Jesus, you are to *deliver this man to Satan for the destruction of the flesh*, so that his spirit may be saved in the day of the Lord" (1 Corinthians 5:4–5, emphasis added). Talk about an awkward church service. *Hey, Gary, we really love you and want God to save your soul, so we're gonna go ahead and hand you over to Accuser-Adversary so he can destroy your flesh.*

It's not the only time Paul enlists Accuser-Adversary for the Lord's service. When two churchgoers named Hymenaeus and Alexander "shipwrecked their faith," Paul reports in 1 Timothy 1:20 that the men have been "handed over to Satan that they may learn not to blaspheme." Were they restored? We don't know, but some think 2 Corinthians 2:5–11 suggests at least one of them was. If this is true, it reveals an epic fail in Christian history: A New Testament church had enough false grace to tolerate the sexual abomination of incest, but had trouble mustering enough real grace to accept back their repentant brother!

When Christians rebel against their King, God hands them over to the enemy for correction. Deuteronomy 28:47–48 says, "Because you did not serve the LORD your God with joyfulness and gladness of heart, because of the abundance of all things, therefore you shall serve your enemies whom the LORD will send against you." Slavery is the inevitable result of rebellion. If you want to understand why the world (including Christians) is mired in debt and suffering compounding economic hardship, it's because the people of God have virtually ignored what the Bible actually has to say about money. Debt, bankruptcy, poverty, inequality—it's all covered in Scripture. Accuser-Adversary is a tool of God not unlike a garden hoe or a wheelbarrow. Ripping out weeds is painful and dirty work but it's an absolute requirement for cultivating God's good garden.

5. *God uses Accuser-Adversary to dispense justice.*

God can and does use evil to do His will. As a way of executing justice for the murder of seventy brothers, "God sent an evil spirit between Abimelech and the leaders of Shechem, and the leaders of Shechem dealt treacherously with Abimelech" (Judges 9:23). After King Saul repeatedly refused to submit to God's ultimate authority, "the Spirit of the LORD departed from Saul, and a harmful spirit from the LORD tormented him" (1 Samuel 16:14). It's the harmful spirit that drives Saul to seek out a lyre player to soothe his mind, which is how God's chosen replacement (the future King David) gets ushered directly into the palace. God allowed evil men like Maximilien Robespierre to lead the French Revolution that guillotined the evil aristocrats who were starving the poor to death.

Before we start accusing God of sinning, let's remember that it is *not* a sin to let evil destroy evil. There is nothing sinful about locking Hitler and Stalin together in a cage match with knives. Only their free will would compel them to sin and kill each other. If my best friend and I were placed in the same situation, we'd use those same knives to start sawing our way to shared freedom. Evil tends to be the snake that eats itself, and it's a great mercy from God that tyrannies inevitably implode. Christians aren't called to root evil out of the world (Matthew 13:24–43). It's far better to just plant good (Mark 4:1–20) and stay out of the fray while evil destroys itself. As Helen Keller put it in *The Story of My Life*, "It is wonderful how much time good people spend fighting the devil. If they would only expend the same amount of energy loving their fellow men, the devil would die in his own tracks of ennui."[2]

God set up the universe so that evil cannot win. Pure, global, eternal totalitarianism simply isn't possible because enduring victory requires unity, and evil is a constant fragmentation. I can think of no better picture of this than the 2001 film *The One*. Jet Li plays a rogue multiverse agent who tries to kill all other versions of himself so he can become an all-powerful god-being. Spoiler alert: The bad guy ends up in a penal colony in the Hades Universe, where he stands atop a ziggurat battling a never-ending stream of throne contenders for all eternity.

6. *God uses Accuser-Adversary to sanctify faithful disciples.*

Paul doesn't just sic Accuser-Adversary on disobedient disciples—he personally submits to God's use of the devil to sanctify him as a Christian apostle. To be sanctified is to be wholly set apart for the Creator's intended use. All Paul cared about was living according to God's plan and purpose, and if that included a lifelong onslaught from Accuser-Adversary, so be it.

> To keep me from becoming conceited because of the surpassing greatness of the revelations, a thorn was given me in the flesh, a messenger of Satan to harass me, to keep me from becoming conceited. Three times I pleaded with the Lord about this, that it should leave me. But he said to me, "My grace is sufficient for you, for my power is made perfect in weakness."
>
> 2 Corinthians 12:7–9

God used Team Accuser-Adversary to keep the apostle Paul from becoming conceited! God also used the devil to prove to Paul that God's grace is sufficient for whatever weakness he suffered. Paul, for his part, takes it phenomenally well. He knows the things he's seen are potential pride points, and he's willing to put up with Accuser-Adversary if it keeps him humble. Paul's response in 2 Corinthians 12:10 is exemplary: "For the sake of Christ, then, I am content with weaknesses, insults, hardships, persecutions, and calamities. For when I am weak, then I am strong." How's that for a judo move? God uses Accuser-Adversary not only to keep history's most influential Christian from sinning, but to make him stronger in the process.

And remember, Paul had anything but smooth sailing through this mortal life:

> Five times I received at the hands of the Jews the forty lashes less one. Three times I was beaten with rods. Once I was stoned. Three times I was shipwrecked; a night and a day I was adrift at sea; on frequent journeys, in danger from rivers, danger from robbers, danger from my own people, danger from Gentiles, danger in the city, danger in the wilderness, danger at sea, danger from false brothers; in toil and hardship, through many a sleepless night, in hunger and thirst, often without food, in cold and exposure. And, apart from other things, there is the daily pressure on me of my anxiety for all the churches.
>
> 2 Corinthians 11:24–28

Paul relates this huge list of horrors in defense of his apostleship—patient endurance amidst suffering serves as proof of his faithfulness to God.

7. *God uses Accuser-Adversary to deliver His witnesses home.*

Perhaps the most sobering of God's uses for Accuser-Adversary is the extrication of Christians from this life so

He can usher them on to the next. Read what Jesus says to the church of Smyrna in Revelation 2:10. "Do not fear what you are about to suffer. Behold, the devil is about to throw some of you into prison, that you may be tested, and for ten days you will have tribulation. Be faithful unto death, and I will give you the crown of life."

The Greek word for witness is *martus*, from whence we get *martyr*. Jesus was serious when He said following Him requires us to pick up a cross (Matthew 16:24). Sin opened the door for death, and God uses Accuser-Adversary and death to free Christians from this world of sin. This is an act of mercy—to cut short their earthly suffering so they can enjoy the delights of eternity with the God they loved more than life itself. Our invitation is to martyrdom—to live (and perhaps even die) bearing faithful witness to the triumph of Christ over sin and death, and sometimes God uses Accuser-Adversary to help us display that faithful witness.

God's ultimate judo move was using Accuser-Adversary's scheme to have Christ crucified. The Messiah's murder backfired in a way the evil one never could have predicted—God made Jesus's devilish death and divine resurrection the very means by which we triumph over Accuser-Adversary and receive salvation.

───────

When Mephistopheles reveals himself as a force of evil to Goethe's *Faust*, he rightly describes himself as "Part of that Power, not understood/ Which always wills the Bad, and always works the Good."[3] As we can see, Accuser-Adversary proves himself to be an extremely capable and useful servant of God. To be sure, he does the things he does not out of the goodness or kindness of his heart, but even his murderous hatred is channeled for God's purposes. That's why it's important to not assume the attacks we face are necessarily diabolical. I can't tell you how many times I've prayed for immediate deliverance at the first signs of trouble. We might want a rapid escape, but God might want a lasting change. That's why it's vital we stick close to Jesus so we can discern God's will versus Accuser-Adversary's will in every situation we face. Paul outlines how exactly to do this in Romans 12:1–2. "Present your bodies as a living sacrifice, holy and acceptable to God, which is your spiritual worship. Do not be conformed to this world, but be transformed by the renewal of your mind, that by testing you may discern what is the will of God, what is good and acceptable and perfect." In other words: Die to self, die to the world, and be reawakened in Christ.

The proper use of Accuser-Adversary is to see his trials and temptations as tests to grow our faith and character. We can use his tests to drive us deeper into the arms of God. Satanic tests are an invitation to obedience and faithfulness instead of rebellion. The devil uses human free will to test whether our love for God is true. The tests of Accuser-Adversary are a clarion call to love. We overcome all tests by loving God and others with everything. Love conquers the world, the flesh, the devil, evil, sin, death, hell, all of it. Plus, we can use Accuser-Adversary to make the unbelieving world confront the reality of evil, and in doing so, point the way to Christ.

What's important to note here is that Accuser-Adversary is a mean old wolf, but his master holds his leash and collar in a vice grip. No wonder the devil is furious and hell-bent on the destruction of all creation—all he can do is bark and snap, and when he does get to take a chomp, his master has a plan for it. My writing mentor, the inestimably talented scribe Mark Buchanan, wrote a book called *Your God Is Too Safe*. It seems to me he should have also written a book entitled *Your Devil Is Too Dangerous*. I'm not saying Accuser-Adversary is weak—we've just built him up into this virtually omnipotent force of evil when he's no such thing. As Christians, our devil is too dangerous if we believe he can possess us. Our devil is too dangerous if we believe he can curse us. Our devil is too dangerous if we believe he can lock us into a Faustian bargain we cannot break by the power of the Holy Spirit. Proportion and perspective are essential. Even a penny can block out the 860,000-mile-wide sun if we put it close enough to our eye. But Accuser-Adversary is smaller than a penny compared with the Son of God. He can't make a single move against a human without God's express consent.

Whether he likes it or not, Accuser-Adversary's primary job is to test and accuse you. If you're like me, this truth leads to this question: What is the point of all this testing?

The Refiner's Fire

A crucible is a vessel usually made from clay or graphite that can resist huge amounts of heat, and with temperatures over 1,400 Fahrenheit you can smelt and separate enduring gold from worthless ore.

Life in this fallen world is undeniably a crucible. Earth is a sweltering pressure cooker of anger, hate, violence, and death. But you can't separate gold from ore with just heat. It requires a reducing agent like coke or charcoal to spark the change. Jesus is the refiner (Malachi 3:3). God allows the heat and uses the devil to act as Christ's reducing agent. When the smelting process is complete, you're left with pure gold and ore that is brittle and crumbly. When the purifying work is done, 24-karat-gold Christians will emerge from the rubble.

This purifying theme pops up all over the Bible:

> **Zechariah 13:9:** "I will put this third into the fire, and refine them as one refines silver, and test them as gold is tested."
>
> **First Peter 1:6–7:** "You have been grieved by various trials so that the tested genuineness of your faith—more precious than gold that perishes though it is tested by fire—may be

found to result in praise and glory and honor at the revelation of Jesus Christ."

Proverbs 17:3: "The crucible is for silver, and the furnace is for gold, and the LORD tests hearts."

Proverbs 25:4–5: "Take away the dross from the silver, and the smith has material for a vessel; take away the wicked from the presence of the king, and his throne will be established in righteousness."

Proverbs 27:21: "The crucible is for silver, and the furnace is for gold, and a man is tested by his praise."

Malachi 3:3: "He [Jesus] will sit as a refiner and purifier of silver, and he will purify the sons of Levi and refine them like gold and silver, and they will bring offerings in righteousness to the LORD."

Daniel 11:35: "Some of the wise shall stumble, so that they may be refined."

Daniel 12:10: "Many shall purify themselves and make themselves white and be refined, but the wicked shall act wickedly. And none of the wicked shall understand, but those who are wise shall understand."

If we need inspiration for trusting God in times of trial, testing, and temptation, listen to this beautiful declaration of faith in Job 23:8–10 (emphasis added). "Behold, I go forward, but he is not there, and backward, but I do not perceive him; on the left hand when he is working, I do not behold him; he turns to the right hand, but I do not see him. But he knows the way that I take; *when he has tried me, I shall come out as gold.*"

The point of all our testing is to create everlasting gold. One of the most haunting passages in the Bible is 1 Corinthians 3:10–15.

Let each one take care how he builds. For no one can lay a foundation other than that which is laid, which is Jesus Christ. Now if anyone builds on the foundation with gold, silver, precious stones, wood, hay, straw—each one's work will become manifest, for the Day will disclose it, because it will be revealed by fire, and the fire will test what sort of work each one has done. If the work that anyone has built on the foundation survives, he will receive a reward. If anyone's work is burned up, he will suffer loss, though he himself will be saved, but only as through fire.

We waste far too many of the precious minutes God has given us. What eternal gold are we allowing God to create in our lives? Of all our hours and decades of flitting to and fro, what will last forever? Of all the work and toil, how much will stand the test of time? These questions should disturb us.

We can use Accuser-Adversary as an unwilling ally. When his temptations come, we can choose to see them as tests allowed by God. In other cases, it might be God himself doing the testing. Other times it's neither God nor Accuser-Adversary testing us, particularly when we choose to test ourselves. Recently, I've been testing the strength of my core by seeing how many sit-ups this old body can do. We're told to do the same thing with our spiritual strength. Second Corinthians 13:5 says, "Examine yourselves, to see whether you are in the faith. Test yourselves. Or do you not realize this about yourselves, that Jesus Christ is in you?—unless indeed you fail to meet the test!"

Why are we working so hard? What are we building toward? We need to constantly be testing our work and motives to see if they have any real eternal value. I have a note in golden yellow on top of my daily schedule that reads, "Everything will pass through the fire. Create gold today." In the famous words of the missionary Charles Thomas Studd, "Only one life, 'twill soon be past, only what's done for Christ will last."

The good news is that we are able to buy eternal gold directly from the refiner himself. Jesus says to the church in Laodicea,

I know your works: you are neither cold nor hot. Would that you were either cold or hot! So, because you are lukewarm, and neither hot nor cold, I will spit you out of my mouth. For you say, I am rich, I have prospered, and I need nothing, not realizing that you are wretched, pitiable, poor, blind, and naked. I counsel you to buy from me gold refined by fire, so that you may be rich, and white garments so that you may clothe yourself and the shame of your nakedness may not be seen, and salve to anoint your eyes, so that you may see.

Revelation 3:15–18

We buy eternal gold refined by fire every time we take the breathlessly temporary things of earth—things like time, energy, and money—and invest them in good works for the kingdom of Jesus. There is no better investment allocation possible than to convert earthly coin for eternal gold. The ancient Greeks had a far better grasp of this than we do. For them, there were two types of time: *chronos* and *kairos*.

Chronos is the ticking clock, from whence we get *chronology*. Kairos is a moment of opportunity, the source of all human action and creative endeavor. Unsurprisingly, the Bible is more interested in kairos than chronos, with kairos appearing 500 times in the Greek Bible versus the 317 appearances of chronos.

Chronos is earthly time, kairos is eternal time. Chronos is second time, kairos is sacred time. Chronos is measured in minutes, while kairos is measured in moments of meaning. Chronos is quantitative; kairos is qualitative. Chronos is a date; kairos is destiny. Chronos eventually kills you, whereas Christ-centered kairos endures forever.

Jesus's first recorded public words in Mark 1:15 are a declaration of eternal gold: "The time [kairos] is fulfilled, and the kingdom of God is at hand; repent and believe in the gospel."

When we allow God to turn chronos into kairos by smelting kingdom gold from earthly ore, earth looks more like heaven.

Let us not grow weary of doing good, for in due season [kairos] we will reap, if we do not give up. So then, as we have opportunity [kairos], let us do good to everyone, and especially to those who are of the household of faith.

Galatians 6:9–10

Look carefully then how you walk, not as unwise but as wise, making the best use of the time [kairos], because the days are evil.

Ephesians 5:15–16

In his book *Kaironomia*, Eric Charles White defines kairos as a "passing instant when an opening appears that must be driven through with force if success is to be achieved."[4] The apostle Paul urges us to seize the moment: "Behold, now is the favorable time [kairos]; behold, now is the day of salvation" (2 Corinthians 6:2).

This is why we must pass the tests that God, the world, the flesh, and Accuser-Adversary send our way. James 1:12 says, "Blessed is the man who remains steadfast under trial, for when he has stood the test he will receive the crown of life, which God has promised to those who love him." God's invitation is to use all times of testing to turn temporary chronos trouble into eternal kairos gold by pushing back the empire of darkness and gaining ground for the kingdom of light.

11

THE END

Part One

Grandma said, don't let him fool ya.
He bring up your past, boy, bring up his future.

—Andy Mineo, Chris Mackey, Josep Prielozny
Kevin Burgess, Jaco Cardec, "Not Today Satan"

IN THE LATE FIRST CENTURY, a Christian named John was exiled to the Greek island of Patmos during the persecutions of the Roman emperor Domitian (Revelation 1:9). Perhaps on a Sunday (Revelation 1:10), Jesus sends His personal angel to John (Revelation 1:1) and gets John to write down what he sees. Christians throughout history have considered this a genuine revelation to John by Jesus, which is why the final book in the library of Scripture is called the Revelation.

The Revelation starts with a series of exhortative letters to churches in Asia, then it goes interstellar. Every page of the Revelation is about Jesus, but it's also packed with wild imagery and probable allusions to the Roman Empire. John does his best to describe what he sees, but one wonders if some sections aren't a real glimpse of the future. Is that a nuclear detonation in Revelation 8:8–9? Is that a bioterror weapon in Revelation 8:10–11? Are those robot soldiers in Revelation 9:7–9, or is that a helicopter or drone fleet in Revelation 9:10–11? We simply don't know.

The end of days breaks down into a few major events, though not necessarily in this order: the great tribulation, the rapture and/or second coming, the millennium, and the final judgment. Let's wade into this wild, weird, and wonderful apocalyptic book, but with a major caveat: You need to read the conclusion to discover if this vision is about the past, present, or future. (Also, a spoiler alert: Things don't end well for Accuser-Adversary.)

The Great Tribulation Part One

People face trials and tribulations all the time, but the Revelation suggests there's another tribulation that's so much larger in scope and scale that Christians have called it the great tribulation based on Revelation 7:14 (and for some, Matthew 24:21). It is a season of severe testing for humanity as God unleashes a series of twenty-one judgments for humanity's rebellion. The tribulation is set over a period of seven years, broken into two three-and-a-half-year periods. It's extremely hard to wrap one's mind around the massive tribulation John envisions, so I'll lay it out as best I can.

John sees a scroll. The scroll has seven seals on it. There is a lamb (Jesus). Every time he opens a seal, it unleashes something on humanity.

Seal Judgment #1: "A white horse! And its rider had a bow, and a crown was given to him, and he came out conquering, and to conquer" (Revelation 6:2).

Seal Judgment #2: "Another horse, bright red. Its rider was permitted to take peace from the earth, so that people should slay one another, and he was given a great sword" (Revelation 6:4).

Seal Judgment #3: "A black horse! And its rider had a pair of scales in his hand. And I heard what seemed to be a voice in the midst of the four living creatures, saying, 'A quart of wheat for a denarius, and three quarts of barley for a denarius, and do not harm the oil and wine!'" (Revelation 6:5–6).

Seal Judgment #4: "A pale horse! And its rider's name was Death, and Hades followed him. And they were given authority over a fourth of the earth, to kill with sword and with famine and with pestilence and by wild beasts of the earth" (Revelation 6:8).

Seal Judgment #5: "I saw under the altar the souls of those who had been slain for the word of God and for the witness they had borne. They cried out with a loud voice, 'O Sovereign Lord, holy and true, how long before you will judge and avenge our blood on those who dwell on the earth?' Then they were each given a white robe and told to rest a little longer, until the number of their fellow servants and their brothers should be complete, who were to be killed as they themselves had been" (Revelation 6:9–11).

Seal Judgment #6: "There was a great earthquake, and the sun became black as sackcloth, the full moon became like blood, and the stars of the sky fell to the earth as the fig tree sheds its winter fruit when shaken by a gale. The sky vanished like a scroll that is being rolled up, and every mountain and island was removed from its place. Then the kings of the earth and the great ones and the generals and the rich and the powerful, and everyone, slave and free, hid themselves in the caves and among the rocks of the mountains, calling to the mountains and rocks, 'Fall on us and hide us from the face of him who is seated on the throne, and from the wrath of the Lamb, for the great day of their wrath has come, and who can stand?'" (Revelation 6:12–17)

Revelation 7 is a two-vision interlude before the seventh seal. The first vision is of God protecting a remnant of 144,000 faithful followers, 12,000 from each of the twelve tribes of Israel. The second vision is of a great multitude of people from all nations. These are the survivors of the great tribulation. The pair of visions serve as a hopeful promise that God will save a remnant of humanity despite the destruction caused by sin.

Seal Judgment #7: "When the Lamb opened the seventh seal, there was silence in heaven for about half an hour. Then I saw the seven angels who stand before God, and seven trumpets were given to them. And another angel came and stood at the altar with a golden censer, and he was given much incense to offer with the prayers of all the saints on the golden altar before the throne, and the smoke of the incense, with the prayers of the saints, rose before God from the hand of the angel. Then the angel took the censer and filled it with fire from the altar and threw it on the earth, and there were peals of thunder, rumblings, flashes of lightning, and an earthquake" (Revelation 8:1–5).

Immediately following the opening of the seventh seal come seven angelic trumpeters:

Trumpet Judgment #1: "The first angel blew his trumpet, and there followed hail and fire, mixed with blood, and these were thrown upon the earth. And a third of the earth was burned up, and a third of the trees were burned up, and all green grass was burned up" (Revelation 8:7).

Trumpet Judgment #2: "The second angel blew his trumpet, and something like a great mountain, burning with fire, was thrown into the sea, and a third of the sea became blood. A third of the living creatures in the sea died, and a third of the ships were destroyed" (Revelation 8:8–9).

Trumpet Judgment #3: "The third angel blew his trumpet, and a great star fell from heaven, blazing like a torch, and it fell on a third of the rivers and on the springs of water. The name of the star is Wormwood. A third of the waters became wormwood, and many people died from the water, because it had been made bitter" (Revelation 8:10–11).

Trumpet Judgment #4: "The fourth angel blew his trumpet, and a third of the sun was struck, and a third of the moon, and a third of the stars, so that a third of their light might be darkened, and a third of the day might be kept from shining, and likewise a third of the night" (Revelation 8:12).

As you can see, the judgments are getting more intense, like the pangs of childbirth. The Wormwood passage always fascinated me as a boy—something falls from the sky and poisons a third of the earth's water? What could cause such a thing? Various commentators have suggested anything from a meteorite or comet to a nuclear missile or even a fallen angel/demon, but my guess is this is some sort of bioterror weapon.

I'm purposely taking a bit of a break from the trumpet action right now because John includes a bit of a break in the action too. This is where many theologians believe the second part of the great tribulation starts because of John's warning in Revelation 8:13, "Then I looked, and I heard an eagle crying with a loud voice as it flew directly overhead, 'Woe, woe, woe to those who dwell on the earth, at the blasts of the other trumpets that the three angels are about to blow!'"

The Great Tribulation Part Two

Trumpet Judgment #5: The release of Abaddon/Apollyon.

"And the fifth angel blew his trumpet, and I saw a star fallen from heaven to earth, and he was given the key to the shaft of the bottomless pit. He opened the shaft of the bottomless pit, and from the shaft rose smoke like the smoke of a great furnace, and the sun and the air were darkened with the smoke from the shaft. Then from the smoke came locusts on the earth, and they were given power like the power of scorpions of the earth. They were told not to harm the grass of the earth or any green plant or any tree, but only those people who do not have the seal of God on their foreheads. They were allowed to torment them for five months, but not to kill them, and their torment was like the torment of a scorpion when it stings someone. And in those days people will seek death and will not find it. They will long to die, but death will flee from them.

In appearance the locusts were like horses prepared for battle: on their heads were what looked like crowns of gold; their faces were like human faces, their hair like women's hair, and their teeth like lions' teeth; they had breastplates like breastplates of iron, and the noise of their wings was like the noise of many chariots with horses rushing into battle. They have tails and stings like scorpions, and their power to hurt people for five months is in their tails. They have as king over them the angel of the bottomless pit. His name in Hebrew is Abaddon, and in Greek he is called Apollyon.

The first woe has passed; behold, two woes are still to come" (Revelation 9:1–12).

Trumpet Judgment #6: "Then the sixth angel blew his trumpet, and I heard a voice from the four horns of the golden

altar before God, saying to the sixth angel who had the
trumpet, 'Release the four angels who are bound at the great
river Euphrates.' So the four angels, who had been prepared
for the hour, the day, the month, and the year, were released
to kill a third of mankind. The number of mounted troops
was twice ten thousand times ten thousand; I heard their
number. And this is how I saw the horses in my vision and
those who rode them: they wore breastplates the color of
fire and of sapphire and of sulfur, and the heads of the
horses were like lions' heads, and fire and smoke and sulfur
came out of their mouths. By these three plagues a third of
mankind was killed, by the fire and smoke and sulfur coming out of their mouths. For the power of the horses is in
their mouths and in their tails, for their tails are like serpents
with heads, and by means of them they wound.

The rest of mankind, who were not killed by these
plagues, did not repent of the works of their hands nor
give up worshiping demons and idols of gold and silver
and bronze and stone and wood, which cannot see or
hear or walk, nor did they repent of their murders or
their sorceries or their sexual immorality or their thefts"
(Revelation 9:13–21).

Let's note how hard-hearted humans become toward the end
of days. Imagine if four armies from the Middle East containing 200 million soldiers (demonic soldiers, robot soldiers, human
soldiers in exoskeletons?) joined together and murdered a third of
humanity. You'd think the rest of the world would turn to God,
but instead, people double down in their sin. Are all of these hap-
penings literal and physical, or are they symbols in John's dream
state? Only God knows. Prophecy has three major elements: revelation, interpretation, application. We can make best guesses, but
the reality is that we're probably overshooting or undershooting
both the physical and spiritual dimensions of this heady revelation.

John takes another pause in the action from Revelation 10 to Revelation 11:1–14 before the seventh trumpet sounds. In this interlude are seven thunders (which John doesn't write down), a little scroll (which John eats), and two witnesses who are murdered by the beast but then come back to life. Once again, God protects His remnant amidst the chaos and destruction.

Trumpet Judgment #7: "Then the seventh angel blew his trumpet, and there were loud voices in heaven, saying, 'The kingdom of the world has become the kingdom of our Lord and of his Christ, and he shall reign forever and ever.' And the twenty-four elders who sit on their thrones before God fell on their faces and worshiped God, saying,

'We give thanks to you, Lord God Almighty,
    who is and who was,
for you have taken your great power
    and begun to reign.
The nations raged,
    but your wrath came,
    and the time for the dead to be judged,
and for rewarding your servants, the prophets and saints,
    and those who fear your name,
    both small and great,
and for destroying the destroyers of the earth.'

Then God's temple in heaven was opened, and the ark of his covenant was seen within his temple. There were flashes of lightning, rumblings, peals of thunder, an earthquake, and heavy hail" (Revelation 11:15–19).

Seven judgment scrolls down, seven judgment trumpets down, seven judgment bowls to go. But first, another interlude.

In Revelation 12, a dragon (presumably Accuser-Adversary) tries to attack a pregnant woman (presumably Israel) and eat her newborn baby (presumably Jesus), but God once again rescues His remnant. Things get even crazier in verses 7–12.

> Now war arose in heaven, Michael and his angels fighting against the dragon. And the dragon and his angels fought back, but he was defeated, and there was no longer any place for them in heaven. And the great dragon was thrown down, that ancient serpent, who is called the devil and Satan, the deceiver of the whole world—he was thrown down to the earth, and his angels were thrown down with him. And I heard a loud voice in heaven, saying, "Now the salvation and the power and the kingdom of our God and the authority of his Christ have come, for the accuser of our brothers has been thrown down, who accuses them day and night before our God. And they have conquered him by the blood of the Lamb and by the word of their testimony, for they loved not their lives even unto death. Therefore, rejoice, O heavens and you who dwell in them! But woe to you, O earth and sea, for the devil has come down to you in great wrath, because he knows that his time is short!"

This is the great reveal that suggests the Eden serpent and Accuser-Adversary are one and the same, and that satan-devil-dragon are all the same being. Up until this moment, there has been a place for Accuser-Adversary and his demons in the court-room of heaven, but no longer. In Jude 9, Michael did not fight Accuser-Adversary, but now he girds his loins and goes to war *in heaven*, the former colleagues now battling violently.

This leads to a lot of confusion for some people, because Jesus said way back in John 12:31, "Now is the judgment of this world; now will the ruler of this world be cast out." In Luke 10:18, after Jesus' disciples subdued demons in His name, Jesus also said, "I saw Satan fall like lightning from heaven." Was Jesus having a vision of the future? Is John mistaken? Or does Accuser-Adversary regularly get booted from heaven for various and sundry courtroom violations, and now this time it's permanent? We don't know, but it seems most likely that, to the moment I write these words, Accuser-Adversary still has access to heaven to accuse Christians day and night, but someday, his pass will be permanently revoked.

Accuser-Adversary first lashes out at Israel and Jesus (Revelation 12:13–16), and when God protects them, he stalks after Christians instead (Revelation 12:17). Accuser-Adversary is furious now that he's permanently locked out of heaven and decides to unleash hell on earth. Some people believe this is the second three and a half years of the seven-year tribulation. He starts by trying to replicate the Trinity—Accuser-Adversary the dragon father, the beastly Antichrist son with his "resurrected" head (Revelation 13:3), and a second beast/false prophet whose job is to get people to worship the Antichrist beast. The Antichrist is not like all the other antichrists we see in the Bible and in the world today. By this point in the judgment cycle, non-Christians around the world will be ready to give god status to anyone or anything who can unite the entire world.

World domination has been humanity's dream from time immemorial. Think of how many times we've tried to establish global control: The Greek Empire, the Persian Empire, the Roman Empire, the Holy Roman Empire, the Mongol Empire, the Spanish Empire, the French Empire, the British Empire, the Third Reich, the Soviet Union, the American empire, the United Nations, the European Union. Now we're seeing the rise of the Chinese Empire with its Belt and Road Initiative global debt trap, and the corporatist finance empire with its transnational, anti-national, anti-democratic, Mammon-worshiping agenda. Global unity (or subjugation) has been the dream of humanity since the building of the Tower of Babel (Genesis 11:4), but never for the right motives and certainly not under submission to the right King. The great irony of all empire builders is that unity proves impossible. The quest for power attracts power-loving opportunists, who are inevitably and happily prone to stab each other in the back at the first sign of weakness. The skill set required to build empires—endless greed, unquenchable power-lust, unfathomable violence—are the same qualities that bring all empires to their knees.

Yet, for a period of forty-two months, the Antichrist beast will accomplish what no leader in history has ever done: unify the world and stabilize the global economy. We don't know what the Antichrist beast will look like, but Revelation 13:1 suggests it will be a confederacy of ten nations that declares war against Christianity and subjugates "every tribe and people and language and nation" (Revelation 13:7). Expect the most unity the world has ever known—one world religion, one world government, one global economy, one unified science, and one universal philosophy, all coalesced in one entity. Many a man has called himself Messiah or Emperor before, but this fellow will genuinely be both. The problems of the world will appear to cease, all thanks to this new religio-socioeconomic system: the Pax Satana. Resistance will not be strong. The world loves sin, and the vast majority of people will be happy to follow along, and true Christians won't be going around murdering soldiers of the new world reich.

Let's briefly speculate how one entity could unify the whole world. By the year 2200, there will likely be more than 10 billion people living on planet Earth, almost exclusively in cities and hyper-cities. Out of the 7,000 languages spoken today, there may only be a few dozen living languages left (think English, Mandarin, Spanish, French, Hindi, etc.) with most people speaking English or Mandarin as a second language. Considering AI can already take an online video and dub it in hundreds of languages using the original author's voice, expect instant language translation technology to allow every person on earth to communicate. We may or may not achieve Elon Musk's Neuralink—nor do I deem its benefits to the few worth the costs to the rest—but the Internet will continue to enmesh humanity toward a singular networked super-brain.

Let's recap what's happened in the Revelation so far: We've had war. We've had hyperinflation. We've seen famine and disease hit a quarter of the earth. We've had a bigger earthquake than any in history. A third of the earth is scorched by hail-fire. A third of the fish and the ships in the sea are destroyed. Some kind of poison affects a third of all rivers and springs. There's some sort of volcano that blocks out the sun, and some sort of five-month metallic locust-scorpion-horse-lion army attack. Four countries on the waters of the Euphrates (Turkey, Syria, Iraq, and Iran?) amass an army of 200 million soldiers and murder a third of humanity. Accuser-Adversary has been ejected from heaven and is tormenting earthlings 24/7. And now an entity has risen to bring order to all this chaos. It appears, at first, the beast is inanimate (perhaps a supercomputer?). Revelation 17:12–13 suggests ten nations choose ten new leaders who immediately delegate their authority to the Antichrist beast. Little do they know they're all being played, because Revelation 17:17 says, "God has put it into their hearts to carry out his purpose by being of one mind and handing over their royal power to the beast, until the words of God are fulfilled." Though the Antichrist beast may be inanimate at the start, Revelation 13:11–15 suggests a second beast-entity called the false prophet (possibly comprised of two smaller nations) takes control of the entity after showing off some incredible new powers or technologies. The false prophet creates an image of the beast and gives it the ability to both speak and slay those who refuse to worship its image. Perhaps a respected deceased figure will be "reanimated" with advanced hologram technology or as a physical AI humanoid; we don't know. Second Thessalonians 2:9–10 suggests Accuser-Adversary will use false signs and wonders to help the false prophet and the Antichrist beast spread the lie of human godhood and self-sovereignty without the need for God.

It seems reasonable that the door to world domination will open through the global economic system. At present, a French-based conglomerate can impoverish sugar farmers in Brazil through suppressing wages, and a Chinese-based monopoly can impoverish Canadians by buying up dairy farms and oil pipelines.

Trillion-dollar hedge funds like Blackstone can impoverish Swedish tenants through ever-rising rents, and multi-trillion-dollar American banks like JPMorgan Chase can devastate tens of millions of would-be homeowners through the evils of interest. Control of the global financial network is key. The entity in charge of a quantum computer with AI machine learning could theoretically parse all numbers on planet Earth and make things immediately fair, or at least popular with the majority. It could tax all rents and interest out of existence, factor in the full cost of pollution, drive corporate efficiency to 100 percent by driving corporate profit to 0 percent, and ensure everyone on earth truly has enough to survive and thrive. In other words, it would have the power to enact socio-enviro-economic sustainability, which would be extremely welcome in a world of climate catastrophes, species collapse, and resource wars.

But at what cost? A hive-mind super-economy would almost certainly weaponize a global central bank digital currency (CBDC) that could be created, taxed, controlled, and surveilled at all times. The entity would dictate how money could and couldn't be spent. It could instantly bankrupt any dissenter. It could enlist and deploy decentralized and autonomous paramilitaries to quell resistance the way Uber enlists extra drivers at rush hour. Revelation 13:16–17 explicitly says the entity will require everyone to bear its mark, perhaps a chip implant, "so that no one can buy or sell unless he has the mark."* The Greek word for mark here is *charagma*, meaning stamp or engraving, not unlike the coins of ancient Rome and today. This mark will contain the name of the entity or his symbolic number. The number in question is 666, which we will

---

* This is why it is imperative for Christians, churches, and denominations to buy as much land as possible, starting immediately. Not only can we steward it now to generate the blessings of food and shelter for those in need, but when no one can buy and sell goods and services without the mark of the Antichrist beast, being able to generate food and shelter outside the money system will be essential for the physical survival of Christians so they can continue to spread the gospel.

note is *not* Accuser-Adversary's number. Revelation 13:18 says very clearly that 666 is the number of a man, not a devil.

So what does 666 represent? Plenty of weird and wonderful theories have been put forward. Perhaps it's a reference to the richest man on earth in 1 Kings 10:14, Solomon, who receives 666 talents of gold each year. God creates the earth in six days and rests on the seventh, so if seven represents God's perfection, then six represents man's fallenness and 666 means "not God, not God, not God." If 777 is the perfect system, then perhaps 666 represents humanity's false religions, false politics, and false economics. If you add up all the consecutive integers from one to thirty-six (i.e., 1 + 2 + 3 etc.) you get 666, so maybe 666 just represents the inevitable conclusion of humanity's continuous rebellion.

In 1 Samuel 17:4–7, Goliath is six cubits (and a span) in height, has six pieces of armor, and his spear's head weighs 600 shekels, so perhaps 666 means any seemingly insurmountable foe of the most high God. In Daniel 3:1–6, King Nebuchadnezzar's golden image is sixty cubits high and six cubits wide, and he makes the people play six specific instruments as they worship his image. John 6:66 is a story about the mass rejection of Jesus. First John 2:15–17 uses the word *world* six times. Perhaps John is using gematria* (a cipher in which numbers represent letters) to encode emperor Nero's name without getting in trouble. Perhaps Nero is just a representation of all powers aligned with Accuser-Adversary in his quest for world domination. And 666 might mean all of these or none of these. We just don't know. But clearly, 666 is an extremely archetypal number associated with rebellion against God.

---

* If you're looking for a wee bit of nonsense entertainment when you finish reading this book, go online and find a gematria calculator. According to Gematrix .org, Jared Brock in Hebrew gematria is 835, which is the same number as "Not Afraid of Truth," "I am Human Suit of God," "Solomons key," "Pruning The Tree Of Life," "Unlimited Greatness," "Death for the Son of Satan," "Try CBD For Pain," and quite hilariously, "Meaning of Numbers in the Bible."

Revelation 14 sees three angels warn humanity to repent of their rebellion, followed by a harvest of the righteous and unrighteous. Revelation 15 sees seven angels ready seven bowls containing seven plagues. It's hard to believe that everything up to now was just a warm-up, but now comes the time of God's wrath. Clearly, as shown in Revelation 16, He takes sin and evil and rebellion far more seriously than we do.

Bowl Judgment #1: "So the first angel went and poured out his bowl on the earth, and harmful and painful sores came upon the people who bore the mark of the beast and worshiped its image" (Revelation 16:2).

Bowl Judgment #2: "The second angel poured out his bowl into the sea, and it became like the blood of a corpse, and every living thing died that was in the sea" (Revelation 16:3).

Bowl Judgment #3: "The third angel poured out his bowl into the rivers and the springs of water, and they became blood. And I heard the angel in charge of the waters say,

'Just are you, O Holy One, who is and who was,
    for you brought these judgments.
For they have shed the blood of saints and prophets,
    and you have given them blood to drink.
It is what they deserve!'

And I heard the altar saying,

'Yes, Lord God the Almighty,
    true and just are your judgments!'" (Revelation 16:4–7)

Bowl Judgment #4: "The fourth angel poured out his bowl on the sun, and it was allowed to scorch people with fire. They were scorched by the fierce heat, and they cursed the name of God who had power over these plagues. They did not repent and give him glory" (Revelation 16:8–9).

Bowl Judgment #5: "The fifth angel poured out his bowl on the throne of the beast, and its kingdom was plunged into darkness. People gnawed their tongues in anguish and cursed the God of heaven for their pain and sores. They did not repent of their deeds" (Revelation 16:10–11).

Bowl Judgment #6: "The sixth angel poured out his bowl on the great river Euphrates, and its water was dried up, to prepare the way for the kings from the east. And I saw, coming out of the mouth of the dragon and out of the mouth of the beast and out of the mouth of the false prophet, three unclean spirits like frogs. For they are demonic spirits, performing signs, who go abroad to the kings of the whole world, to assemble them for battle on the great day of God the Almighty. ('Behold, I am coming like a thief! Blessed is the one who stays awake, keeping his garments on, that he may not go about naked and be seen exposed!') And they assembled them at the place that in Hebrew is called Armageddon" (Revelation 16:12–16).

Bowl Judgment #7: "The seventh angel poured out his bowl into the air, and a loud voice came out of the temple, from the throne, saying, 'It is done!' And there were flashes of lightning, rumblings, peals of thunder, and a great earthquake such as there had never been since man was on the earth, so great was that earthquake. The great city was split into three parts, and the cities of the nations fell, and God remembered Babylon the great, to make her drain the cup of the wine of the fury of his wrath. And every island fled away, and no mountains were to be found. And great hail-stones, about one hundred pounds each, fell from heaven on people; and they cursed God for the plague of the hail, because the plague was so severe" (Revelation 16:17–21).

Revelation 17 and 18 see the judgment of "Babylon," the city that represents all false systems of religion, politics, and economics.

All told, the great tribulation is going to be brutal—far worse than the Holocaust and the Holodomor combined. Jesus says in Matthew 24:21 that "there will be great tribulation, such as has not been from the beginning of the world until now, no, and never will be." What is the purpose of this tribulation? It is first and foremost a pouring out of God's wrath and judgment on a world in rebellion, but it's also a season of hardcore refinement for the Christian church (whether all the Christians or the new post-rapture converts, depending on how things actually play out). The creation of diamonds takes unfathomable heat, pressure, and time, but what emerges is pure, beautiful, and unbreakable. The body of Christ will be tested by Accuser-Adversary, the Antichrist beast, the false prophet beast, and a world of lies, manipulation, coercion, and violence, but God will bring His people through the fire and all the way to the Marriage Supper of the Lamb in Revelation 19.

I should note that there are some theologians who believe the great tribulation has already happened. This view is called *preterism*. Their idea is that much or most of Revelation is symbolic of the pain and suffering experienced by the Jewish people when their temple, city, and nation were destroyed by the Roman Empire under Emperor Titus in 70 AD. The belief that the great tribulation will happen in the future is called *futurism*, and the belief that the tribulation is slowly and currently unfolding over time is called *historicism*. If you think that's confusing, just wait until you hear about the rapture.

12

THE END

Part Two

"Awake, arise or be for ever fall'n."

—John Milton, *Paradise Lost*

The Rapture

There are several passages that suggest Christians will, at some point, be taken up to heaven while the rest of the world carries on. Paul envisions it this way: "Behold! I tell you a mystery. We shall not all sleep, but we shall all be changed, in a moment, in the twinkling of an eye, at the last trumpet. For the trumpet will sound, and the dead will be raised imperishable, and we shall be changed" (1 Corinthians 15:51–52).

We don't know when, exactly, the Day of the Lord will happen. In fact, not even Jesus knows (Matthew 24:36), but says His return will hit earth like a Noachic flood (Matthew 24:37–39). "Two men will be in the field; one will be taken and one left. Two women will be grinding at the mill; one will be taken and one left" (Matthew 24:40–41).

The Revelation itself doesn't have much to say about the rapture, though some see whispers of it, especially Revelation 3:10, which says, "Because you have kept my word about patient endurance, I will keep you from the hour of trial that is coming on the whole world, to try those who dwell on the earth."

There's also a serious battle among Bible nerds as to whether the rapture will happen before, during, or after the great tribulation. These three camps even have names for themselves: Pre-tribulationists, Mid-tribulationists, and Post-tribulationists.

Pre-tribulation rapture

The most famous of the pre-tribbers are John MacArthur and David Jeremiah, along with novelists Jerry Jenkins and Tim LaHaye, whose *Left Behind* books sold 60 million copies in the wake of 9/11. Their proof text is 1 Thessalonians 4:15–17.

> For this we declare to you by a word from the Lord, that we who are alive, who are left until the coming of the Lord, will not precede those who have fallen asleep. For the Lord himself will descend from heaven with a cry of command, with the voice of an archangel, and with the sound of the trumpet of God. And the dead in Christ will rise first. Then we who are alive, who are left, will be caught up together with them in the clouds to meet the Lord in the air, and so we will always be with the Lord.

Some pre-trib theologians believe the rapture will lead to the salvation of thousands of Jews during those turbulent seven years. MacArthur envisions the tribulation as a time of massive upheaval and spiritual awakening, and certainly the disappearance of upward of a billion Christians would cause instant global chaos, as well as an openness to spirituality like never before in history. As the old dad joke goes, some people are so pre-trib that they refuse to eat Post cereal. Even if all the Christians are raptured before the great tribulation, it appears some folks will get saved during this time. Expect Jewish Christians to be at the center of the resistance. Hatred for Jewish Christians seems to reach its zenith at the battle of Armageddon, a war that may start in the Valley of Megiddo but not end until it engulfs the whole Middle East and beyond.

Mid-tribulation rapture

Mid-tribulationists believe Jesus will swoop up all the Christians halfway through the great tribulation. They go all the way back to Daniel 9:27 for support and then tie it to Matthew 24:15–41 to make the argument plausible. They also cite 1 Corinthians 15:51–52 and tie it to the last of the seven trumpets of Revelation 11:15–19, which they believe will blare during the middle of the tribulation. Mid-tribbers believe the rapture takes place between the opening of the sixth and seventh seals of the scroll, because the signs seem eerily similar to the second coming of Christ mentioned in Matthew 24:29–30. Mid-tribbers also believe the seventh seal represents raptured Christians who've been rescued from the great tribulation before the Antichrist's arrival. Put another way, mid-tribbers believe the rapture is the end of the church's tribulation and the start of the world's tribulation.

Post-tribulation rapture

Post-tribulationists (including John Piper, John Stott, Wayne Grudem, R. C. Sproul, and N. T. Wright) believe Jesus will come to collect all the Christians at the end of the seven-year great tribulation. This fits well with Scripture's overall theme of Christians suffering for the gospel, and having a faithful Christian witness endure straight through the hardest testing in human history brings more glory to God and His church. Post-tribbers often note the fuzzy distinction between the rapture and the second coming in the Bible, and many believe the rapture and the second coming may very well be one and the same.

No matter which way you lean—pre-trib, mid-trib, or post-trib—I think we can all agree that the tribulation is going to be an exceedingly trying time for Christians. How will these Christians overcome Accuser-Adversary? Revelation 12:11 lists three things: "They have conquered him by the blood of the Lamb and by the word of their testimony, for they loved not their lives even unto death." If you want to know how Christians conquer Accuser-Adversary, it all comes down to Jesus's sacrifice, their personal testimony of His saving grace, and not loving their lives in the face of martyrdom. Mercifully, all tribbers agree that even the seven-year great tribulation eventually comes to an end.

The Second Coming

The end starts with what seems like "the voice of a great multitude" roaring like water and thunder in heaven (Revelation 19:1, 6). In perhaps the strangest scene imaginable, the saints let out a declaration of victory and sit down to tuck into a marriage feast *before* going to battle to defeat the forces of darkness. That's how powerful God is compared with Accuser-Adversary, and how full of faith the church is compared with the world. Christ is the Lamb, and the church of Christ is the radiant bride adorned in fine linen representing the righteous works of Christians. Party first, battle later.

The battle takes place in Revelation 19:11–16.

Then I saw heaven opened, and behold, a white horse! The one sitting on it is called Faithful and True, and in righteousness he judges and makes war. His eyes are like a flame of fire, and on his head are many diadems, and he has a name written that no one knows but himself. He is clothed in a robe dipped in blood, and the name by which he is called is The Word of God. And the armies of heaven, arrayed in fine linen, white and pure, were following him on white horses. From his mouth comes a sharp sword with which to strike down the nations, and he will rule them with a rod of iron. He will tread the winepress of the fury of the wrath of God the Almighty. On his robe and on his thigh he has a name written, King of kings and Lord of lords.

Matthew 25:31 and 2 Thessalonians 1:7 say angels will join Jesus in this final invasion, and "fine linen, bright and pure" is the phrase used in Revelation 19:8 to describe what Christians will be wearing. Will the people of Jesus follow Christ and His angels into battle against the ten-nation Antichrist entity-beast and all the other rebellious armies of earth? I dearly hope so.

Once again, victory is declared before the battle actually starts. "Then I saw an angel standing in the sun, and with a loud voice he called to all the birds that fly directly overhead, 'Come, gather for the great supper of God, to eat the flesh of kings, the flesh of captains, the flesh of mighty men, the flesh of horses and their riders, and the flesh of all men, both free and slave, both small and great'" (Revelation 19:17–18).

Jesus also depicts this event in Matthew 24:29–31.

Immediately after the tribulation of those days the sun will be darkened, and the moon will not give its light, and the stars will fall from heaven, and the powers of the heavens will be shaken. Then will appear in heaven the sign of the Son of Man, and then all the tribes of the earth will mourn, and they will see the Son of Man coming on the clouds of heaven with power and great glory. And he will send out his angels with a loud trumpet call, and they will gather his elect from the four winds, from one end of heaven to the other.

The battle itself lasts just three verses, from Revelation 19:19–21.

And I saw the beast and the kings of the earth with their armies gathered to make war against him who was sitting on the horse and against his army. And the beast was captured, and with it the false prophet who in its presence had done the signs by which he deceived those who had received the mark of the beast and those who worshiped its image. These two were thrown alive into the lake of fire that burns with sulfur. And the rest were slain by the sword that came from the mouth of him who was sitting on the horse, and all the birds were gorged with their flesh.

As far as we know, the Antichrist beast-entity and its false prophet beast-entity will be the first two entrants to the lake of fire. They won't be the last.

The Millennium

Revelation 20:1–6 envisions what would surely be the greatest thousand-year period of human history prior to the end of this age.

> Then I saw an angel coming down from heaven, holding in his hand the key to the bottomless pit [Greek *abyssou,* abyss] and a great chain. And he seized the dragon, that ancient serpent, who is the devil and Satan, and bound him for a thousand years, and threw him into the pit, and shut it and sealed it over him, so that he might not deceive the nations any longer, until the thousand years were ended. After that he must be released for a little while.
>
> Then I saw thrones, and seated on them were those to whom the authority to judge was committed. Also I saw the souls of those who had been beheaded for the testimony of Jesus and for the word of God, and those who had not worshiped the beast or its image and had not received its mark on their foreheads or their hands. They came to life and reigned with Christ for a thousand years. The rest of the dead did not come to life until the thousand years were ended. This is the first resurrection. Blessed and holy is the one who shares in the first resurrection! Over such the second death has no power, but they will be priests of God and of Christ, and they will reign with him for a thousand years.

How awesome does that sound? Instead of the tyranny of dictatorship, monarchy, oligarchy, and sham democracy, humanity could experience ten centuries of Christ-led theocracy.

When, exactly, this takes place is another matter for debate in which Bible nerds split off into one of three camps:

A. Pre-millennialists believe Jesus will return before His literal thousand-year reign on Earth, but are split on whether the rapture will happen before, during, or after the great tribulation.

B. Post-millennialists believe Jesus won't gather all the Christians until after the seven-year tribulation and a symbolic millennium where the Christian church spreads the gospel to all nations and ushers in a long era of peace and prosperity.

C. Amillennialists, like post-millennialists, believe the word *millennium* is just a symbolic term, but instead of looking forward to a future golden era, amillennialists believe Jesus is already reigning both in heaven and in the hearts of Christians. We're currently living in that "millennium"—Christ is on His heavenly throne, all dead Christians are in heaven with him, and the kingdom of God is advancing on earth. Some amillennialists don't like being called amillennialists because it makes it seem as though they don't believe in the millennium reign of Christ. They prefer the rather beautiful term *realized millennialism*, or *now-millennialism*. There is no rapture in amillennialism—when Christ comes back, He will set up His kingdom for all time.

What or when the millennium may be has been a debate among Christians for thousands of years, with all sides believing theirs is the right camp, despite arguments that can be made in all directions. It would be dogmatism and fundamentalism to not have grace and patience with each other over an issue that is clearly unclear. Fortunately, the millennium is an open-handed issue, not a make-or-break gospel salvation question.

But that certainly hasn't stopped folks throughout history from making definitive claims about said millennium:

- Multiple German emperors of the Holy Roman Empire claimed to be the final emperor preparing the way for Christ's thousand-year reign.
- Martin Luther, in turn, believed the Catholic papacy was the antichrist, so surely the thousand years were soon at hand.
- In his book *The Thousand Years of the Apocalypse*, Thomas R. Sharp interprets the millennium as lasting from Charlemagne's Carolingian Renaissance to the French Revolution.
- A radical group of English Puritans called themselves the Fifth Monarchy Men because they believed the four empires mentioned in Daniel and Revelation had fallen and it was high time for Christ to establish His throne.
- Christopher Columbus believed his job was to spread the gospel to the New World before the whole world ended in 1656.
- David Koresh, the founder of a Waco-based splinter cult of the Seventh-Day Adventists, believed he was God's final prophet and that he would soon rule with Christ.
- The founder of the Jehovah's Witnesses believed the millennium started in 1874 and that Christ would return in 1914, though how exactly that short window of time equaled a thousand years is beyond me.

Until the end of the world, there will always be people who predict the end of the world.

Has the thousand years already happened or not? There is not a fallen human on earth who can say definitively. If pre-millennialism is correct (and I'm not saying it is or isn't), and there is a literal thousand-year reign of Christ, shall we briefly touch on where Accuser-Adversary will be spending his more or less 365,250 days in captivity? There's much confusion surrounding hell, the lake of fire, Sheol, Hades, and the abyss—let's try to sort it out while the professional Christians bicker about the millennium for the next thousand years.

Sheol

Sheol is mentioned sixty-six times in the Old Testament, and it simply means underworld. It's the shadowy underplace where everyone went when they died, whether they believed in God or not.

Sheol is not somewhere away from God's presence. Proverbs 15:11 says, "Sheol and Abaddon lie open before the LORD." Job 26:6 says, "Sheol is naked before God, and Abaddon has no covering." Psalm 139:8 says, "If I ascend to heaven, you are there! If I make my bed in Sheol, you are there!" Sheol isn't permanent. Job at a low point says, "He who goes down to Sheol does not come up" (Job 7:9), but 1 Samuel 2:6 says God "brings down to Sheol and raises up," plus Jonah is rescued from Sheol in Jonah 2:2.

Hades

Hades is the Greek word for Sheol, but with a bit more nuance. Jesus's parable in Luke 16:19–31 seems to hint that Hades has at least two compartments between which "a great chasm has been fixed, in order that those who would pass from here to you may not be able, and none may cross from there to us" (v. 26). The poor man Lazarus now rests on Abraham's bosom, while the rich man is tormented by fire and thirst. Yet the pair can communicate as though side-by-side. It's a very strange story, to be sure.

Hades, like Sheol, is not separated from the presence of God.

Hades, like Sheol, is not a permanent residence but more of a temporary stay. "And the sea gave up the dead who were in it, Death and Hades gave up the dead who were in them" (Revelation 20:13).

Some scholars believe every person of faith who died pre-Christ just chilled out in Hades, and that when Jesus ascended into heaven, He took them with Him (Ephesians 4:8). At the very least, Christ's death swung the gates of heaven wide open, because Jesus actually tells the repentant thief on the cross behind Him that on that very day he will enter Paradise (Luke 23:43). A short while later, while Stephen was being stoned and becoming Christianity's first martyr, he saw Jesus waiting for him in heaven (Acts 7:55).

While we can't say for certain, some argue that those imprisoned in Sheol/Hades prior to the advent of Christ might still get a chance to know the risen Savior. "Christ also suffered once for sins, the righteous for the unrighteous, that he might bring us to God, being put to death in the flesh but made alive in the spirit, in which he went and proclaimed to the spirits in prison, because they formerly did not obey" (1 Peter 3:18–20). But I would caution against "second chance" theology because it's a quick and slippery slide into full-blown universalism.*

What is certain is who owns Hades—Jesus. "I died, and behold I am alive forevermore, and I have the keys of Death and Hades" (Revelation 1:18). What's also certain is how Hades finishes its life cycle. "Then Death and Hades were thrown into the lake of fire. This is the second death, the lake of fire" (Revelation 20:14).

Abyss

The abyss is mentioned nine times in the New Testament and it simply means bottomless. This one seems to be reserved

---

* For a good read on this, see The Gospel Coalition article "Does 1 Peter 3:19 Teach That Jesus Preached in Hell?" by Guy Waters.

specifically for evil spirits including the Beast (Revelation 11:7) to be held until their time has come. The legion of demons in Luke 8:31 beg Jesus not to send them to the abyss.

The angel of the abyss is a king called Abaddon in Hebrew and Apollyon in Greek (Revelation 9:11), but the key to the abyss is given to an angel of heaven in Revelation 9:1 and Revelation 20:1. Revelation 9:2 describes the abyss much like a volcano. "He opened the shaft of the bottomless pit, and from the shaft rose smoke like the smoke of a great furnace, and the sun and the air were darkened with the smoke from the shaft." This is where Accuser-Adversary will be imprisoned for 1,000 years (Revelation 20:3) if the millennium is a literal thousand-year period.

Tartarus

Tartarus is mentioned only once in the Bible and it's a term borrowed from Greek mythology. Tartarus was the lowest possible part of the underworld, residing somewhere below Hades. In Peter's conception, Tartarus might just be another name for abyss, as it similarly functions as a holding cell for evil spirits. "For if God did not spare angels when they sinned, but cast them into hell [Tartarus] and committed them to chains of gloomy darkness to be kept until the judgment" (2 Peter 2:4).

Hell

Hell is mentioned twelve times in the New Testament, and all but one mention are connected to strong warnings by Jesus against sinning (e.g., Mark 9:43–48). The Greek word for hell is *geenna*, the English *Gehenna* being the vile valley near Jerusalem where rebellious kings of Judah once immolated their own children in worship to Moloch (2 Chronicles 28:3).

Is hell just another word for Sheol/Hades/abyss? Is it a separate place? Is it not a real place at all, but rather a potent earthly image of a real spiritual place called the Lake of Fire? The Bible doesn't say for certain. Sheol, Hades, abyss, Tartarus, death, and hell might be six individual places or they might all be the same thing—we just don't know.

Lake of Fire

The lake of fire is mentioned four times in the Bible, though all mentions of hell bear a striking resemblance. In the Matthew 13:42 parable of the wheat and weeds, the master instructs his servants to "throw them into the fiery furnace. In that place there will be weeping and gnashing of teeth." This lake of fire was not originally created for humans. The Matthew 25:41 parable of the goats and sheep ends with "Then he will say to those on his left, 'Depart from me, you cursed, into the eternal fire prepared for the devil and his angels.'" The first three entrants to the lake of fire will be the Antichrist beast, the false prophet, and Accuser-Adversary (Revelation 19:20; Revelation 20:10).

Unfortunately, we humans, like sheep, have gone astray (Isaiah 53:6), and without righteousness through faith in Christ, we too are marked for the lake of fire. "As for the cowardly, the faithless, the detestable, as for murderers, the sexually immoral, sorcerers, idolaters, and all liars, their portion will be in the lake that burns with fire and sulfur, which is the second death" (Revelation 21:8). "If anyone's name was not found written in the book of life, he was thrown into the lake of fire" (Revelation 20:15).

This brings us to eternal conscious torment, known by many as "that hideous doctrine" that children of God cannot think about without being driven to tears, prayer, and action. Does eternal conscious torment violate the love of God? Doesn't it contradict the Romans 6:23 idea that the wages of sin is death? Is the lake of fire permanent or temporary? How could a physical body burn for eternity without being destroyed? Or how could a physical fire burn a spiritual body? Does biblical justice require God to punish finite sins infinitely? Does God's justice, wrath, grace, or love get the final word?

The idea that God will simply end the consciousness of all damned humans and other spirits (including Accuser-Adversary) is called *annihilationism* or *terminal punishment*. There's also *universalism* or *restoration*, the belief that everyone will be saved. One can also be a partial annihilationist, believing God will end the consciousness of all damned humans but eternally torment Accuser-Adversary and his minions.

There are verses that seem to support the notion of eternal conscious torment (Matthew 25:46; Revelation 14:11), verses that seem to support the view of terminal punishment (Matthew 10:28; John 3:16; Philippians 3:19) and verses that could go either way (Revelation 20:14–15; Mark 9:48; Isaiah 66:24). Does 2 Thessalonians 1:9, "They will suffer the punishment of eternal destruction, away from the presence of the Lord and from the glory of his might," mean eternally being destroyed or destroyed forever? If God is eternal and omnipresent, how can someone be eternally separated from His presence except by total destruction? There's also the possibility that immortality is not part of humanity's fallen nature and that only Christ can make a person live forever (Romans 2:7; 1 Corinthians 15:53–54; 1 Timothy 6:15–16; 2 Timothy 1:10).

From our limited human perspective, everlasting immolation seems disproportionate to *any* sin, even the worst imaginable acts. The punishment doesn't seem to fit the crime. But we cannot forget that God is a God of justice, and not the kind of "justice" that rich corporations can buy in today's courtrooms. The Great Judge genuinely knows all the facts, considers all the evidence, even knows every motive and inner thought. No matter what punishment awaits unbelievers—be it eternal conscious torment, annihilation, or something in between—the result will be pure and perfect justice. Grace and pardon were already offered and rejected. Perhaps we find the lake of fire so repulsive because of our desensitization to sin. This should leave us rightly terrified. We can't say for certain what happens to unbelievers when they die, but the discussion itself should massively elevate our awe of God and our hatred of sin.

Mercifully, avoiding an eternity separated from the presence of God isn't difficult. All we have to do is follow Jesus and avoid committing the unpardonable sin.

The Unpardonable Sin

There is only one sin that God cannot forgive: continued rebellion in the form of rejecting His offer of salvation. To blaspheme the Holy Spirit—to show contempt in thought, word, or deed and resist the work of God's invitational presence—is to eternally cut oneself off from grace (Matthew 12:31–32; Mark 3:28–30; Luke 12:10). For Christians, there's no such thing as unpardonable sin because Christians do not blaspheme the Holy Spirit. Our eternity is secured in Christ.

Becoming a Christian is, at its core, dead simple: "Believe in the Lord Jesus, and you will be saved" (Acts 16:31). A Christian is someone who genuinely believes Jesus is the Son of God and God the Son, and the fruit of that belief is a life spent with Jesus, becoming like Jesus, and doing the things Jesus did (Matthew 7:16). This life-changing belief is the difference between an eternity spent in the presence of God or forever cut off from it. Our righteousness before God is our faith in Jesus, nothing more, nothing less. All we have to do is receive His invitation of salvation. As John 1:12 puts it, "To all who did receive him, who believed in his name, he gave the right to become children of God."

Satan Sprung

For those who believe in a literal thousand-year reign, Accuser-Adversary spends one thousand years in the abyss. Is this God's last grace-filled attempt to reform and restore him? Some have suggested so, but I strongly doubt it, and either way, it doesn't work. When the millennium ends in Revelation 20:7–8, Accuser-Adversary immediately rallies a world army from nations across the globe and marches against the camp of Christians and Jerusalem. Evidently humanity and Accuser-Adversary learned nothing after a long season of Christian reign. This time, the battle is over before it begins. In fact, the enemy army's demise doesn't even get a whole verse, just a few words: ". . . but fire came down from heaven and consumed them" (Revelation 20:9).

So what was the point of an extended test run of Christian rule? I think it's so humanity can see our total fallenness. That even without any interference or suggestions or temptations from Accuser-Adversary and his demons, humans will *still* choose rebellion and self-will over the kingship of Christ. G. K. Chesterton put it well in *The Hammer of God*, a short story in his collection called *The Innocence of Father Brown*: "'Are you a devil?' 'I am a man,' answered Father Brown gravely; 'and therefore have all devils in my heart.'"[1] Humans are fully capable of sin without Accuser-Adversary. Even if Accuser-Adversary never rebelled against God or never even existed, a free-willed being such as ourselves would have chosen rebellion and opened the door to sin and death. "The devil made me do it" won't fly on Judgment Day.

Revelation 20:10 is the last time we read of Accuser-Adversary in the Bible. "The devil who had deceived them [the nations] was thrown into the lake of fire and sulfur where the beast and the false prophet were [are], and they will be tormented day and night forever and ever." Note the devil and his minions aren't the ones doing the torturing of humans we see in Dante's pitchforked pictures. They're the ones being tormented. Accuser-Adversary's fall happens in three steps: He is cast out of heaven. He is bound for a millennial era. He is cast into the lake of fire. Where, exactly, will Accuser-Adversary spend eternity? "Before the throne there was as it were a sea of glass, like crystal" (Revelation 4:6). "I saw what appeared to be a sea of glass mingled with fire—and also those who had conquered the beast and its image and the number of its name, standing beside the sea of glass with harps of God in their hands" (Revelation 15:2). "If anyone worships the beast and its image and receives a mark on his forehead or on his hand . . . he will be tormented with fire and sulfur in the presence of the holy angels and in the presence of the Lamb. And the smoke of their torment goes up forever and ever, and they have no rest, day or night, these worshipers of the beast and its image, and whoever receives the mark of its name" (Revelation 14:9–11). *The lake of fire is within sight of God.* Rebellionists in eternity will be fully aware of what they missed.

Therein finishes Accuser-Adversary's sordid tale. It is strange to think he and his co-rebels might end up in heaven, in the presence of God, stuck behind some sort of one-way glass mirror. Is the lake of fire's location permanent? Revelation 21 later speaks of a new heaven and a new earth that becomes God's dwelling place but makes no mention of where the lake of fire ends up once evil ceases to exist. Verse 4 says, "He will wipe away every tear from their eyes, and death shall be no more, neither shall there be mourning, nor crying, nor pain anymore, for the former things have passed away." Is the lake of fire a former thing? Verse 8 says, "But as for the cowardly, the faithless, the detestable, as for murderers, the sexually immoral, sorcerers, idolaters, and all liars, their portion will be in the lake that burns with fire and sulfur, which is the second death." Verse 27 says nothing unclean will ever enter the new city of God, which suggests the lake of fire does, at some point, get banished from the presence of God.

When all this will take place is a matter of far too much speculation. You can be a pre-tribulation pre-millennialist, a mid-tribulation pre-millennialist, a post-tribulation pre-millennialist, a post-millennialist, or an amillennialist. In regard to the great tribulation you can also be a preterist, a futurist, or a historicist. We didn't dig into pre-wrath, progressive dispensationalism, optimistic amillennialism, post-millennialist optimism, perfect amillenarism, imperfect amillenarism, or historic premillennialism, because, frankly, even I'm not that big a Bible nerd, and as we'll see in the conclusion shortly, it's probably a trick question.

Jesus's point in Matthew 24:36 remains rock solid: "Concerning that day and hour no one knows." Out of respect for Jesus and a burning desire for unity within the body of Christ, it would be wise not to take a fundamentalist position on any of these possible permutations. My dad calls himself a pan-tribulationist: "God's going to make it all pan out." Humility is the key to any study of the end times. Multiple eschatological events have or will happen, in which exact order no one knows, and God will remain solidly sovereign from start to finish. In the meantime, Jesus explicitly lays out our job in Matthew 24:42, 44–46. "Stay awake, for you do not know on what day your Lord is coming. . . . Therefore you also must be ready, for the Son of Man is coming at an hour you do not expect. Who then is the faithful and wise servant, whom his master has set over his household, to give them their food at the proper time? Blessed is that servant whom his master will find so doing when he comes."

Accuser-Adversary decided to be counted in the number of those found in rebellion at the time of Christ's return, and he will live to regret it for all eternity. So now we return full circle to one of our original questions: What is the testing-tempting Accuser-Adversary's actual name? Was he Lucifer? Satan? Devil? In the end, he doesn't have a name. He is stripped of his titles and roles—he is no longer the light-bearing lucifer, the truth-seeking satan, or the justice-meting devil. Now he's just a serpent, a dragon, a beast. Whatever his glorious name once was, he is now forever nameless, purposeless, and powerless.

That is the end of the story of the devil.

But the end of the devil is not the end of the story.

CONCLUSION

"What a day, glorious day, that will be."

—Jim Hill, "What a Day That Will Be"

I must confess I've done something a bit naughty with the Revelation. Like jamming a square peg into a round hole, I (and a million ministers throughout history) pitched you John's apocalypse as a logical, linear, progressive, beginning-middle-and-end Western book.

But the Revelation is none of those things.

The real reason there's so much hullabaloo over the chronological sequence of the Revelation is that the Revelation is *probably not a chronological story*. My theologian friend Richard John Saunders again: "Revelation is likely a prophetic loop—the events portrayed are the same events over and over."

G. K. Beale, in his *New International Greek Testament Commentary on The Book of Revelation*, points out five of these loops:

Loop #1: Revelation 6:12–17 and Revelation 7:9–17

Loop #2: Revelation 11:18a and Revelation 11:18b

Loop #3: Revelation 14:14–20 and Revelation 15:2–4

Loop #4: Revelation 16:17–21; Revelation 17:1–18:24; and Revelation 19:1–10

Loop #5: Revelation 20:7–15 and Revelation 21:1–8 and Revelation 21:9–22:5

Stunningly, the loops all follow the same pattern:

1. Spirits with free wills (Accuser-Adversary, angels/demons/ devils/antichrists, humans) rebel against the word, will, and way of God and cause damage to themselves, others, and creation.
2. God judges them for their sin.
3. God saves a remnant of faithful and resilient Christians.

Repeat.

Even non-Christians have a deeply intuitive sense of this rebellion-judgment-salvation cycle. In his book *The Changing World Order: Why Nations Succeed and Fail*, billionaire hedge-fund founder Ray Dalio describes a "Big Cycle" of new order, peace and prosperity, inequality and debt, bubbles and crises, depression and revolution. Or perhaps you've heard the quote attributed to G. Michael Hopf in *Those Who Remain*: "Hard times create strong men. Strong men create good times. Good times create weak men. And, weak men create hard times."[1] A perfect example of this was the *trente glorieuses*, the glorious thirty years of relative global peace, economic growth, and rapid rise in middle class living standards following the devastation of World War II. Millions of German, Italian, and Japanese men had waged war against the Imago Dei, and God allowed the Allies to bring horrific judgment on Europe and Asia, but rescued a remnant that rebuilt much of the world.

The rebellion-judgment-salvation cycle has repeated itself throughout all of human history *without exception*. A vast swath of the Old Testament is devoted to this cycle, especially the Histories and the Prophets. Yahweh sends His people into slavery in Egypt and the Babylonian exile because of their rebellion. Yahweh uses Israel to judge Canaan because of its rebellion. Yahweh raises up Samson and the Philistines because "everyone did what was right in his own eyes" (Judges 21:25). Israel is then conquered by Greeks and Rome because of their rebellion. Rebellion, judgment, salvation. Over and over and over again. The rebellion-judgment-salvation cycle teaches us about the horrific nature of our sinful fallenness, the perfect holiness of God, and our utter helplessness to escape the cycle apart from grace through faith.

The Revelation describes the pangs of childbirth. The cycles become more and more intense with each round of contractions. Loop #4 is the most intense judgment in the cycles. Loop #5 is the most intense salvation in the cycles. Female contraction pangs end with the delivery of a baby. So too will God eventually end the rebellion-judgment-salvation cycle with the deliverance of an entirely new reality.

Is the Revelation applicable to the Roman Empire? Absolutely. Is it applicable to the British Empire? Yep. The American empire? For sure. The rising Chinese empire and the global finance corporatocracy? Without a doubt. God brooks zero rebellion, whether it comes from north, south, east, or west. From ancient Assyria to the near-future, corporate-controlled, AI-policed, neo-feudal colonies, judgment is the natural consequence of sin. But God, in His mercy, always preserves a faithful remnant to rise like a phoenix from the ashes of desolation.

The lesson for us is that the Revelation isn't just a vision of the future: It's a glimpse of multiple pasts, multiple presents, and multiple futures that explicitly inform how Christians are to live for God in all times and places.

New Life

Eventually, the painful pangs of the ever-intensifying rebellion-judgment-salvation cycle will reach their conclusion. Head to Revelation 20:11–15. Accuser-Adversary is no more. Earth and sky—and presumably the rest of the physical universe—no longer exist. God is seated on a great white throne, surrounded by open books, including one special book called the Book of Life. All the dead will stand (on what?) before the throne. The sea, death, and Hades all give up their captors, and "the dead were judged by what was written in the books, according to what they had done." The book of life is present, and "if anyone's name was not found written in the book of life, he was thrown into the lake of fire." Some theologians argue the great white throne judgment is exclusively for non-Christians, but nothing in the Revelation passage explicitly states Christians won't be there, and nothing in the passage explicitly states it's only for non-Christians.

What we know for certain is that, for the first time in history, the judgment will be fair. The perfect judge will administer perfect justice. Death and Hades are thrown into the lake of fire, and "if anyone's name was not found written in the book of life, he was thrown into the lake of fire" (v. 15). This group includes "the cowardly, the faithless, the detestable, murderers, the sexually immoral, sorcerers, idolaters, and all liars" (Revelation 21:8).

Jesus describes it this way in Matthew 25:31–33, 41–46:

When the Son of Man comes in his glory, and all the angels with him, then he will sit on his glorious throne. Before him will be gathered all the nations, and he will separate people one from another as a shepherd separates the sheep from the goats. And he will place the sheep on his right, but the goats on the left. . . .

Then he will say to those on his left, "Depart from me, you cursed, into the eternal fire prepared for the devil and his angels. For I was hungry and you gave me no food, I was thirsty and you gave me no drink, I was a stranger and you did not welcome me, naked and you did not clothe me, sick and in prison and you did not visit me." Then they also will answer, saying, "Lord, when did we see you hungry or thirsty or a stranger or naked or sick or in prison, and did not minister to you?" Then he will answer them, saying, "Truly, I say to you, as you did not do it to one of the least of these, you did not do it to me." And these will go away into eternal punishment, but the righteous into eternal life.

In Revelation 21, God gifts us a new heaven, a new earth, and a new jewel-encrusted Jerusalem with a street of glasslike gold. The street has a river running down the middle of it, with a single tree of life rooted on both banks, yielding a different fruit each month. In this new reality, death, pain, even sadness no longer exist. Neither does the sun or moon, because God's glory is more than bright enough. There is also no temple in this new city, because God himself is the temple. In verse 3, a voice booms from the throne: "Behold, the dwelling place of God is with man. He will dwell with them, and they will be his people, and God himself will be with them as their God."

The "End" of Free Will

Will free will exist in heaven? Will people be allowed to still rebel against God like Accuser-Adversary did? Eternity is a long time to remain faithful. (One imagines that even the most loving of spouses could not make it last for eternity.) After a few trillion years, won't we eventually become like the devil and try to set ourselves up as God? What is to stop humans from disobeying or rebelling against God, if only for a moment?

Some people believe we'll always have the option to choose rebellion. Others posit that we'll still have free will, but God will write His law on our hearts (Jeremiah 31:33–34) and radically alter our desires and eliminate all reasons to sin.

Folks have posed different solutions to the question of how we will remain faithful to God forever. Perhaps He will perform a spiritual lobotomy and remove our free will? This seems unlikely, as turning us into automatons would remove our ability to truly love God, though one could also argue that free will is itself part of the fall and the source of rebellion.

Paul, for his part, doesn't even bother to speculate and just throws his hands in the air with joyous trust. "Now we see in a mirror dimly, but then face to face. Now I know in part; then I shall know fully, even as I have been fully known" (1 Corinthians 13:12).

Will we sign a golden scroll forfeiting our free will? There are some earthly precedents for this idea:

- Before undergoing surgery under anesthetic, patients of their own volition must temporarily surrender their free will to the surgeon.
- My last act of free will was getting married to Michelle. From that day forward, she had claims on my freedom.
- When someone becomes a Christian, that's technically their last act of free will too.
- Even Jesus said of His Father, "Not my will but yours be done."

Perhaps when we get to heaven, we'll choose to forever sign over our free will to God's will (ideally with a Carrie Underwood country song playing in the background—"Jesus, Take the Wheel"). Would you let your last act of free will be to eternally entrust your free will to God's will? I think it would be a bet worth taking.

That said, I don't think we'll actually need to sign away our free will. We'll be so utterly transformed that the very thought of rebellion is unthinkable. Philippians 3:21 says Jesus "will transform our lowly body to be like his glorious body." First Corinthians 15:52 says that "the dead will be raised imperishable, and we shall be changed." First John 3:2 backs it up: "Beloved, we are God's children now, and what we will be has not yet appeared; but we know that when he appears we shall be like him, because we shall see him as he is." If we become like Jesus in every way, all potential for sin and rebellion will simply cease to exist.

Here's an additional thought to ponder. In addition to changing our very nature, I believe God will continue to reveal new aspects of His character and glory—facets Accuser-Adversary never experienced—revelations so overwhelming and all-consuming, so intoxicating as to keep us in perpetual awe of His glory and forever in love with Him for all of eternity. How this is possible I don't know, because I'm not God. I still have a few tricks up my sleeve to impress my wife and kids in the future, but God has planned an eternity of delights for you. Several verses support this supposition. Psalm 145:3 says God's greatness is unsearchable. First Corinthians 2:9 says, "What no eye has seen, nor ear heard, nor the heart of man imagined, what God has prepared for those who love him." The following verse (1 Corinthians 2:10) suggests that promise is also available in the *here and now*, so imagine what it will be like in the *there and then*. Perhaps the best case to be made for God forever blowing us away with His awesomeness is made in Ephesians 2:6–7, where it says God has "raised us up with him and seated us with him in the heavenly places in Christ Jesus, so that in the coming ages he might show the immeasurable riches of his grace in kindness toward us in Christ Jesus."

So allow yourself to balloon with anticipation. You cannot burst. You cannot overhype heaven or set your expectations too high. For the first time in your entire life, you will experience total and everlasting fulfillment, completeness, wholeness, oneness.

In this new world, Christians reign with God "forever and ever" (Revelation 22:5) as a kingdom of priests (Revelation 1:5–6). Unlike the violence-enforced "peace" of past empires like the Pax Romana, the Pax Britannia, and the Pax Americana—all ultimately fallen member states of the Pax Satana—finally, we will live in a permanent heavenly kingdom with a universal vision for humanity, a worldview where active love reigns for all time.

Welcome to the *Pax Christiana*.

AFTERWORD

Writing *A God Named Josh* was a joy and pleasure. Writing a "biography" on Accuser-Adversary was something of another order. Unlike Jesus of Nazareth, Accuser-Adversary of Heaven is not a historical human personage who incarnated in a physical body in first-century Judea or any other time or place before or after. Eyewitness testimonies are nonexistent, hearsay is plentiful, and opposition is fierce.

From the week we decided to embark on this book, life went into a tailspin of chaos. Our apartment bloomed with mold. Our wealthy tax-exile landlords refused to fix the problem. As we recovered from mold exposure, we were sick more times in the following year than from all illnesses suffered in the previous *decade*. Due to the housing crisis, we found ourselves unable to secure a rental in our town and had to move into a friend's spare room for a year. Michelle developed a painful nerve condition and numbness for which specialists have yet to find a source or a cure. I developed a skin condition across my face and had multiple dental problems. We were gazumped on a house purchase and lost nearly a thousand dollars. We eventually bought a house after months of delays, discovered a false wall with a rotten floor behind it the next day, and were drained of our savings overnight. An algorithm change evaporated my main source of income in less than four weeks. I slept poorly for the first time in my life and had strange dreams, including one of a dead man in a coffin who sat up, opened his tuxedo, and revealed himself to be a green cobra. I suffered a debilitating back injury that has left me unable to sit, stand, or walk without pain. This led to sciatica arcing electric lightning bolts of nerve pain down my right calf. I've never been late on delivering a manuscript, but twice had to push my deadline on this one and had to work straight through Christmas Day to get it done. Even the edits were plagued with problems: files that wouldn't open, surprise house repairs, and home Internet that simply stopped working. It has been the worst season in (but mercifully not of) our married lives. Our watchwords became *patient endurance*, and we weren't sure how much more we could bear. It was, in a very real sense, the year from hell.

But we got off easy compared with the makers of *The Omen* film series. They dodged two flights struck by lightning, a plane crash, and an Irish Republican Army (IRA) bombing. The special-effects artist who designed the film's famous decapitation scene was shortly thereafter involved in a car accident in which his passenger was decapitated. Similarly harrowing stories have been reported on the making of *The Exorcist* and *Rosemary's Baby* films.

To be fair, the year I spent writing this book was also a time of great blessing. Our baby boy became a happy toddler and veritable carnivore whose first phrase was "more beef." One of my teenaged Sunday school kids got to see her best friend come to Christ, and God allowed me to lead one of the teen boys to Jesus. We became debt-free home stewards, thanks to the Acts 2 generosity of a small group of radical Christians.

My work on this volume is now done, and I am relieved this test is over. As I hope you now see, *A Devil Named Lucifer* is actually a book about Jesus. The devil is not the main character in God's history or your story. Ironically, the devil is a minor player even in his own biography. As we've seen, Satan is not the only satan, the devil is not the only devil, and if he was a former lucifer, he's certainly not a lucifer now, and is not the Lucifer. Lucifer, Satan, the Satan, Devil, the devil, Accuser-Adversary, call him what you will, but he only definitively appears five times in the entire Bible. He accuses and tests Job, he accuses Joshua, he tests Jesus, he enters Judas, and he is punished for his sins. He only speaks on five occasions, mostly quoting and misquoting Scripture while fulfilling his role as tester and accuser. He's barely present, he barely speaks, he's not described as we picture him, he's not in charge of hell, and though he's an adversarial tester on earth and accuser in heaven, he's still a servant of God. By the end of the story, the perhaps-once-luciferous-now-satanic devil not only doesn't have a role to play for all eternity—he doesn't even have a name. He, like all former things including sin, pain, sadness, and death, will not even be a distant memory in eternity. All that will remain is the manifest presence of God dwelling with His people forever.

So, perhaps Accuser-Adversary is a cautionary tale of what it means to rebel against the King and His kingdom. This book is an invitation to accept God's sovereignty—His now and eternal dominion over everything and everyone.

May His kingdom come.

May His will be done.

On earth as it is in heaven.

Soli deo gloria.

Glory to God alone.

May the true "lucifer"—Jesus the risen Son, the light of the world—rise radiantly in your hearts.

ACKNOWLEDGMENTS

Thanks first to Andy McGuire and the whole team at Bethany House for their encouragement, support, and patience as I trudged through the most difficult project I've ever undertaken. Micah Kandros nailed the design brief. Steph Smith is a joy to work with. Sharon Hodge is an especial gift to the Christian publishing industry at large and my writing in particular.

I am blessed to know some of the greatest biblical minds alive today. Profound thanks to Richard Saunders, Gord Brock, Christopher Frost, Ray Paul, Stu Thompson, and Michael VanEgmond for your generous theological reviews.

Thanks to Dave and Mandy McSporran for your sacrificially generous agape. Ditto Chris and Kate Frost on the hospitality front, and Michelle, my love, on the home front.

ENDNOTES

Chapter 4: The Pointy Red Devil

1. Image generated by DALL·E 3, OpenAI, October 21, 2023, at https://www.bing.com/images/create/.

2. As quoted in Joseph Turmel, *The Life of the Devil* (United Kingdom: Knopf, 1929), 144.

3. As quoted in Norman Cohn, *Europe's Inner Demons: An Inquiry Inspired by the Great Witch-Hunt* (New York: Basic Books, 1975), 22.

4. Tucker Max, *Assholes Finish First* (New York: Gallery Books, 2010), 321.

5. Charles Baudelaire, *The Prose Poems and La Fanfarlo*, trans. Rosemary Lloyd (Oxford, UK: Oxford University Press, 1991, 2001), 76.

6. Fulton J. Sheen, *Life of Christ* (New York: Image Books/Doubleday, 1958, 2008), 67.

7. C. S. Lewis, *The Screwtape Letters* by CS Lewis © copyright 1942 CS Lewis Pte Ltd. Extract used with permission.

8. Steven Curtis Chapman with Ken Abraham, *Between Heaven and the Real World: My Story* (Grand Rapids, MI: Revell, 2017), 400.

Chapter 5: In Cahoots with the Devil

1. Pope Gregory I, *Delphi Collected Works of Gregory I* (Hastings, UK: Delphi Classics, 2019), ebook.

2. Johannes P. Louw and Eugene A. Nida, eds., *Greek-English Lexicon of the New Testament Based on Semantic Domains,* vol. 1, *Introduction & Domains* (United States: United Bible Societies, 1988), 147.

3. Martin Luther quoted in Roland Herbert Bainton, *Here I Stand: A Life of Martin Luther* (United Kingdom: Hodder and Stoughton, 1950), 264.

4. Pat Robertson on *The 700 Club*, January 13, 2010, 6:23, https://www2.cbn.com/video/700-club/700-club-january-13-2010.

5. William Blake, *The Marriage of Heaven and Hell: In Full Color* (New York: Dover Publications, 1994), 30.

6. "Remembering Hugo Chavez's U.N. 'Devil Speech'" of September 20, 2006, YouTube, 27 seconds, https://www.youtube.com/watch?v=TLLG9ZEWV6k.

7. Watson Institute for International and Public Affairs, Brown University, "Costs of War," 2024, https://watson.brown.edu/costsofwar/.

Chapter 7: The Devil Incarnate

1. Timothy Keller, "Accuser and the Advocate," sermon, January 29, 2020, *Timothy Keller Sermons Podcast by Gospel in Life*, 10:35, https://podcast.gospelinlife.com/e/accuser-and-the-advocate/.

2. *The Table Talk or Familiar Disclosure of Martin Luther*, trans., William Hazlitt (London: David Bogue, 1848), 30.

Chapter 8: How to Resist the Devil

1. Content condensed and adapted from Thomas Brooks, *Precious Remedies Against Satan's Devices: Being, a Companion for Christians of All Denominations* (Philadelphia: Jonathan Pounder, 1810). This work is in the public domain.

2. Content taken from Erwin Lutzer, *God's Devil: The Incredible Story of How Satan's Rebellion Serves God's Purposes* (Chicago: Moody Publishers, 2015), 50–55. Lutzer lists three lies in this segment. I have reordered and paraphrased them, including them along with some that I wrote, inspired by Lutzer.

3. Lutzer, *God's Devil*. On pages 69–78, Lutzer exposes five lies: reincarnation, esotericism, pantheism, relativism, and hedonism. Here I build on Lutzer's foundation, listing seven lies, with half overlapping his.

4. "Thatch Roofing," *FactRepublic*, n.d., https://factrepublic.com/facts/45194/.

5. Brooks, *Precious Remedies*, 312.

6. Timothy Keller, *Encounters with Jesus: Unexpected Answers to Life's Biggest Questions* (New York: Penguin, 2015), 122.

Chapter 9: The Reason for Evil

1. David Hume, *Dialogues Concerning Natural Religion* (London, 1779), 186.

2. *Cambridge Dictionary*, s.v. "evil," https://dictionary.cambridge.org/us/dictionary/english/evil.

3. *Oxford English Dictionary*, s.v. "evil," https://www.oed.com/search/dictionary/?scope=Entries&q=evil.

4. *Merriam-Webster's Collegiate Dictionary*, s.v. "evil," https://unabridged.merriam-webster.com/collegiate/evil.

5. Ezra Pound, *Gaudier-Brzeska: A Memoir* (London: John Lane, 1916), 136.

6. "Homily of His Eminence Card. Joseph Ratzinger Dean of the College of Cardinals," Vatican Basilica, April 18, 2005, https://www.vatican.va/gpII/documents/homily-pro-eligendo-pontifice_20050418_en.html.

7. Jared A. Brock, "Americans Have Absolutely Zero Clue What True Freedom Means," *Surviving Tomorrow*, October 12, 2022, https://www.surviving-tomorrow.com/p/americans-have-absolutely-zero-clue.

Chapter 10: The Servant Serpent: How to Use the Devil to Serve God

1. Some content adapted from Erwin Lutzer, *God's Devil: The Incredible Story of How Satan's Rebellion Serves God's Purposes* (Chicago: Moody Publishers, 2015), 127–140. Lutzer describes four ways God uses Satan to achieve His purposes, and Lutzer's list was the basis for my own, which grows to seven.

2. Helen Keller and Annie Sullivan, *The Story of My Life* (New York: Doubleday, 1903), 426.

3. Johann Wolfgang von Goethe, *Goethe's Faust, with Some of the Minor Poems* (United Kingdom: Walter Scott, 1889), 58.

4. Eric Charles White, *Kaironomia: On the Will-to-Invent* (University of California, Berkeley, 1983), 3.

Chapter 12: The End: Part Two

1. G. K. Chesterton, *The Innocence of Father Brown* (London: Cassell, 1911), 258.

Conclusion

1. G. Michael Hopf, *Those Who Remain: A Post-Apocalyptic Novel* (pub. by author, 2016), 18.

JARED BROCK is an award-winning author and director of several films, including PBS's acclaimed *Redeeming Uncle Tom* with Danny Glover. His writing has appeared in *Christianity Today*, *The Guardian*, *Smithsonian*, *USA Today*, *Huffington Post*, *Relevant*, and *TIME*.

CONNECT WITH JARED:

JaredBrock.com

@jaredAbrock

@jaredbrock

Notes on a Devil

PART I: WHAT'S HIS NAME?

_____

_____

_____

_____

_____

_____

_____

_____

_____

_____

_____

_____

_____

PART II: APPEARANCE AND ALLIES

PART III: WORK AND LOCATION

Notes on a Devil

PART IV: REDEMPTION

You May Also Like . . .

With deft, insightful, and humorous strokes, award-winning biographer Jared Brock weaves archaeology, biology, psychology, history, and theology to create a portrait of Jesus we've never seen before. More than just a fascinating biography, *A God Named Josh* seeks to illuminate our Lord from new perspectives that draw you closer to Him.

A God Named Josh